IN SECRET

*In disguise amongst lamas, robbers, and wise men.
A key to the mysteries of Tibet.*

By

THEODORE ILLION

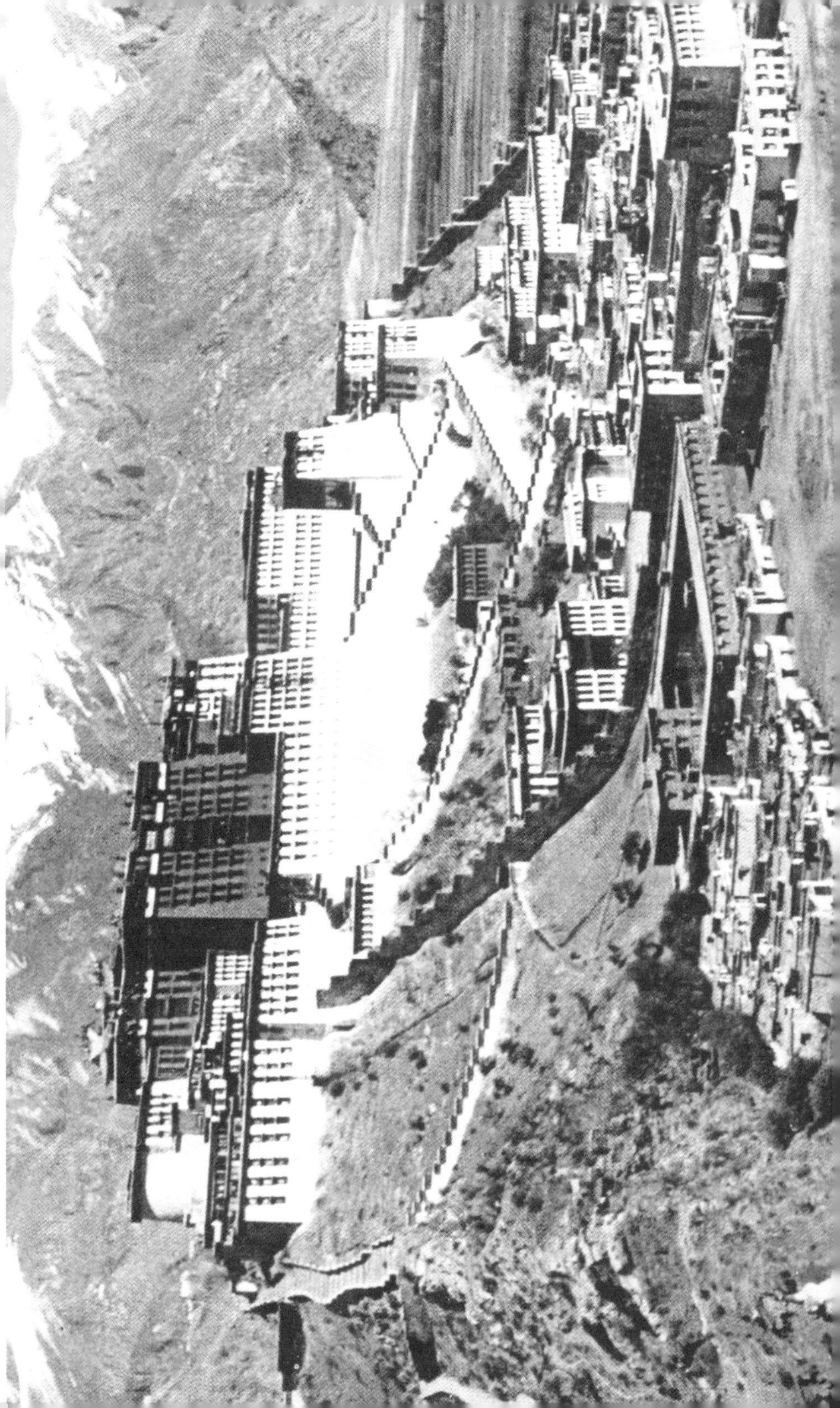

IN SECRET TIBET

T. Illion

In Secret Tibet

Copyright 1937
Theodore Illion

First Published in London by Ryder & Co.

This edition first published 1991

Third printing March 2002

ISBN 0-932813-13-5

Printed in the United States of America

Published by
Adventures Unlimited Press
One Adventure Place
Kempton, Illinois 60946 USA
auphq@frontiernet.net

See us online at:
www.adventuresunlimitedpress.com
www.wexclub.com/aup

The **Mystic Traveller** Series:

- IN SECRET TIBET by Theodore Illion (1937)
- DARKNESS OF TIBET by Theodore Illion (1938)
- IN SECRET MONGOLIA by Henning Haslund (1934)
- MEN & GODS IN MONGOLIA by Henning Haslund (1935)
- MYSTERY CITIES OF THE MAYA by Thomas Gann (1925)
- ALTAI HIMALAYA by Nicholas Roerich (1929)
- IN QUEST OF LOST WORLDS by Byron de Prorok (1937)

SIBERIA
LAKE BAYKAL
Sayan
U.S.S.R.
Altai Mountains
Ulan Bator
Karakorum
MONGOLIA
Dzungaria
ARAL SEA
Syr Darya
Gobi
Alma Ata
Turfan Depression
Kyzyl Kum
Tien Shan
Tarim
Tunhuang
Amu Darya
Samarkand
Fergana
SINKIANG
Kara Kum
Kashgar
Tarim Basin
CHINA
Pamirs
Yarkand
Takla Makan
Khotan
Hindu Kush
Karakoram
Kunlun Mountains
AFGHANISTAN
KASHMIR
TIBET
Indus
Mt. Kailas
Tibetan Plateau
Himalayas
Lhasa
Tsangpo
New Delhi
NEPAL
Mt. Everest
SIKKIM
BHUTAN
Brahmaputra
PAKISTAN
Ganges
Bodhgaya
INDIA
SRI LANKA
0 125 250 500 1000
miles

The Lost Cities Series:
Lost Cities of Atlantis, Ancient Europe & the Mediterranean
Lost Cities of North & Central America
Lost Cities & Ancient Mysteries of South America
Lost Cities of Ancient Lemuria & the Pacific
Lost Cities & Ancient Mysteries of Africa & Arabia
Lost Cities of China, Central Asia & India

The Mystic Traveller Series:
In Secret Mongolia by Henning Haslund (1934)
Men & Gods In Mongolia by Henning Haslund (1935)
In Secret Tibet by Theodore Illion (1937)
Darkness Over Tibet by Theodore Illion (1938)
Danger My Ally by F.A. Mitchell-Hedges (1954)
Mystery Cities of the Maya by Thomas Gann (1925)
The Mystery of Easter Island by Katherine Routeldge (1919)
In Quest of Lost Worlds by Byron de Prorok (1937)

The Atlantis Reprint Series:
Atlantis In Spain by E. M. Whishaw
The History of Atlantis by Lewis Spence
The Riddle of the Pacific by J. M. Brown
The Shadow of Atlantis by Col. A. Braghine
Atlantis Mother of Empires by Stacy Judd
Secret Cities of Old South America by H.T. Wilkins

The Lost Science Series:
UFOs & Anti-Gravity
The Free-Energy Device Handbook
The Anti-Gravity Handbook
Anti-Gravity & the World Grid
Anti-Gravity & the Unified Field
Vimana Aircraft of Ancient India & Atlantis
The Fantastic Inventions of Nikola Tesla by Nikola Tesla
Man-Made UFOs: 1944-1994—50 Years of Suppression

INTRODUCTION:

The German traveller Theodore Illion was one of the first travellers to penetrate Tibet while it was still sealed off from the outside. Illion, who spoke fluent Tibetan, had to disguise himself as a wandering Tibetan monk in order to escape detection, as it was illegal for any foreigner to be in Tibet.

He began planning his trip in 1932 and left Germany in 1934. After several years of adventures and hairaising narrow escapes with death, he returned to Germany to write *Ratfelhaftes Tibet,* published in Hamburg in 1936. His books were quickly translated into English and published by Rider & Company in London: IN SECRET TIBET (1937) & DARKNESS OVER TIBET (1938).

IN SECRET TIBET, a rare book back in print, recounts Illion's preparation for the trip to Tibet and his subsequent meetings with wise hermits once he had illegally entered the country. "This is an armchair travelogue at its very best!"—Bookwatch. The second volume, DARKNESS OVER TIBET, recounts Illion's discovering and entering an underground city.

T. ILLION

PREFACE

Many friends who have listened-in to my numerous broadcasts given in many countries and various languages, have asked me to write a book on the observations and experiences I made and had while studying the spiritual life of Tibet. This book is being published simultaneously in various languages. It is intended for people who want first-hand information about the strange mentality and unexplained phenomena in one of the most mysterious countries in the world.

When this book is read in the East, some readers will no doubt try to dispose of certain irritating truths by calling them "Western" or "Christian" ideas. On the other hand, many an Occidental reader will imagine to have found in this book what he may term Eastern ideas. But TRUTH is neither Occidental nor Oriental and only entirely *unprejudiced* people can grasp it.

I travelled in Tibet neither as a Christian nor as a Buddhist. I did not look at things there merely with the eyes of the scientist or the philosopher. I tried to examine things in an absolutely unprejudiced way. I do not belong

PREFACE

to any sect, party, or denomination. I am merely MAN. And in this book I speak as man to man.

There are readers who wish to amass innumerable details. There are others who look for vital connections which may provide a key to a deeper understanding of this puzzling world of phenomena and everlasting change. The latter may find in this book many a hint enabling them to fathom the mysteries of Tibet.

T. ILLION.

CONTENTS

CHAPTER		PAGE
I.	WHY AND HOW I TRAVELLED IN DISGUISE IN TIBET	13
II.	AMONGST KIND AND HOSPITABLE TIBETAN NOMADS	46
III.	ADVENTURES WITH BRIGANDS	63
IV.	TIBETAN CIVILIZATION	76
V.	THE STRANGE DOINGS OF THE LAMAS	93
VI.	TIBETAN MIRACLES	133
VII.	ETERNAL YOUTH	168

An ancient Stupa (Chorten) near Daithang

IN SECRET TIBET

CHAPTER I

WHY AND HOW I TRAVELLED IN DISGUISE IN TIBET

TIBET, the strange, bleak "roof of the world", is still determined to keep the foreigner out. The trade route from Yatung to Gyangtse is the only part of Tibetan territory really open to foreigners.

Tibet holds many secrets. Strange things, seemingly contrary to all known laws of nature, are reported again and again by the few travellers who have been able to come into close contact with the country and its inhabitants.

Mysteries abound in Tibet. Before visiting it I often wondered whether the strange things reported by quite reliable individuals (who no doubt firmly believed they had witnessed the most extraordinary phenomena) were due to mere hallucination. The first actual unusual experience I had in Tibet could easily have been accounted for by such an explanation.

While spending an icily cold night alone in my tent, I was awakened by ear-piercing cries of pain very similar to the cries of a human being in agony and yet strangely different to any human voice. The sound came from a place that could not have been farther than about forty or fifty yards from my tent. I looked out. It was one of those clear Tibetan nights. The ground was covered with salt crusts reflecting the moonlight. The tent happened to be erected on a gentle slope and the surroundings were such that no man and no animal could hide anywhere within a distance of several hundred yards without being noticed. Notwithstanding this, there was nobody visible. I fell asleep again. Ten minutes later the same shrill and almost human sound of pain was repeated. This time I looked skywards. No bird was visible in the moonlight and, in fact, no small bird could have given utterance to so powerful a cry. When the cry was repeated for the third time I rushed out from the tent in the direction of the strange, ghostly voice. Once more I was baffled. When I had again returned to the tent I heard a somewhat different cry, this time, rather mocking and even exulting, as if making fun of my helplessness.

In the morning I examined the neighbourhood in the hope of finding footprints. There were none! The only footprints I found were my own. These included those I had made during the night.

A man determined to get into really close contact with Tibet and her many secrets must do without most of those comforts that a white person is in the habit of considering as absolutely necessary. For a certain time he must adapt himself entirely to Tibetan conditions, to Tibetan poverty and filth, and to Tibetan standards of living, with all the ensuing lack of comfort. And in many instances the white intruder actually will be worse off than the Tibetans themselves.

But the prospect of closely studying the most mysterious country in the world justifies such a venture.

I had been told that there were some men in Tibet who approximated to the age of six hundred, nine hundred, or even a thousand years. Did such persons exist? What did such venerable gentlemen look like? Was life still worth living for them at such an age? Would they look embarrassed if I asked them to prove their age? Of course, this speculation was based on the assumption that they existed.

I had heard strange stories about white women who were supposed to live in some of the Tibetan monasteries in the company of hundreds of lamas deprived of other female company. How informing it would be to secure an interview with some of these ladies, and ask them to tell me something about their thrilling experiences!

I had read about secret schools in Tibetan monasteries where pupils take an eight years' course in thought-transmission, the pupil and his teacher being seated for weeks or months or years or decades in the same dark room, concentrating on the same mental pictures. Did those schools really exist? Was it possible to develop thought-transmission in this way? Would it be possible for me to get a glimpse of those schools?

And then there were the strange "flying lamas". Did they exist? Would I succeed in meeting and studying at least one of these incredible beings? Other explorers had seen them, and the report of at least one of them was far too detailed and circumstantial to be hastily dismissed.

The *lung-gom-pas* must rightly be described as one of the strangest phenomena that are claimed to exist in Tibet. They do not run, but move past like an elastic ball bouncing off the ground at regular intervals, their arms and legs swinging like a pendulum. Although they move past at a speed of something like fifteen miles an hour

IN DISGUISE IN TIBET 17

they are never out of breath. Their faces are curiously immobile. Their eyes remain wide open and they seem to exist in a strange state of trance.

Small wonder that such extraordinary stories as the above made me desirous to get into really close contact with Tibet, to discover her secrets, although much risk and privation seemed to be inevitable when travelling in disguise in one of the bleakest and least accessible countries in the world.

In Chapter VI of this book, in which I attempt to give an objective and matter-of-fact analysis of Tibetan miracles, I give a description of the *lung-gom-pas* or flying lamas. I met them on two occasions and made the best possible use of the short time during which the phenomenon was visible. The *lung-gom-pas* whom I saw, however, were not loaded up with heavy chains as I expected, on hearing Tibetan stories about them. Their attire was as light in weight as it possibly could have been. The Tibetans say that the flying lamas begin their flying exercises in light clothes, and as they become more familiar with the art of flying they make their clothes heavier, and finally they begin to wind chains round their body to make flying more difficult. I did not see any chains.

But Tibetans often exaggerate. Slight and

insignificant phenomena in Tibet have a tendency to develop into hair-raising and baffling miracles.

In Tibet actual and personal observation is the safest source of information and even then great caution is necessary. One should never mix with a crowd when watching phenomena in Tibet. I never like to mix with crowds and avoid this whenever I can, not merely in the East, but also in the West. Have you ever, while present at a meeting of hundreds of people who happen to think along certain lines, attempted to form thoughts which are diametrically opposed to the ideas of the crowd? Even a sceptical and objective observer is at least subconsciously influenced by his environment, and especially by a crowd. The lamas in Tibet positively delight in crowds. The greater the concourse, the easier things seem to be for the Buddhist priesthood. The lamas dislike the independent thinker. They need flocks.

I had been told that twenty per cent of the population of Tibet were priests and monks. Would I find Tibet a more righteous and pious place than the rest of the world on account of the existence of so many lamas with whom helping others spiritually has become a profession?

So my interest in Tibet was centred around the reality of Tibetan mysteries and psychical phenomena. Unlike some explorers, I was not out for prospecting or gold-hunting. It is true, of course, that Tibet contains a fair quantity of valuable minerals and plenty of gold. Goldwashing is carried on in various parts, and in some rivers gold is so plentiful that very coarse methods of gold-washing yield considerable amounts of gold in a short time. I never really understood why gold is not currency in Tibet. Goods are paid for in copper coins, butter, or barley, but never in gold. On most of the copper coins it is written, by the way, that the Government of the country is a good and victorious one, in order that the Tibetans may not forget it. I wonder why other governments do not adopt this cheap and simple method of self-adulation.

To revert, I did not care a straw for the wealth of Tibet in valuable minerals and gold.

Throughout my travels I carried no arms. Explorers of this type often get into trouble, and perhaps just because I did not go to Tibet for gain I never really got into trouble, although the odds sometimes seemed to be overwhelmingly against me.

Although I am no materialist, I nevertheless start with at least one leg on firm ground. I am not foolhardy. I was fully aware of the fact that such a venture as travelling in disguise in the most inaccessible country in the world necessitated careful training, much preliminary study, and painstaking preparation.

In spite of the admirable work done by a large number of explorers, only a portion of the information and maps required were available. Tibet still remains a *terra incognita* in many respects. For example, her population is estimated at one million and a quarter by some people, and at six millions by others. So ill-defined are her boundaries and her connection with adjacent territories is so vague that her area amounts to between 450,000 and 900,000 square miles, according to what one chooses to consider as belonging to Tibet.

A large portion of Tibetan territory is entirely unmapped. There are white spots on the map covering tens of thousands of square miles, and even the mapped portion varies considerably, making the use of the existing maps very difficult. Besides, there are rapid physical changes. Many lakes shrink from year to year. Frequent and very violent earthquakes alter the surface of the earth. But no matter whether you know your exact location or not you are in perhaps the strangest country in the world. Almost every moment one meets with something new, something unexpected. This makes life there really worth living. Is not the absence of certainty the greatest asset in life?

IN DISGUISE IN TIBET 21

How to get to Tibet?

Foreigners are unwelcome. The dislike of the foreigner seems to be encouraged by the lamas. There are no other countries where twenty per cent of the population live as priests at the expense of the remaining eighty per cent as they do in Tibet. So the less the Tibetans get into contact with foreigners and the less they know about other countries, the better for the lamas.

But there is yet another reason why foreigners are kept out. Every time a foreign expedition visits Tibet, trouble follows.

The Tibetans are convinced that bad thoughts cause disease and that the bad thoughts of white people poison their country. Be that as it may, it is a fact that almost every time expeditions of white people have visited Tibet, some disaster has followed. The Tibetans declare that their presence offends the Tibetan gods and that their evil thoughts cause disease. In any case the Tibetans know *by experience* that disasters follow the coming of white expeditions. To be on the safe side, they bar expeditions altogether. If their hands are forced and they find themselves confronted by a *fait accompli* or if they are coerced into granting a permission, they take good care that the movements of the foreigners should be watched carefully and that people in the districts visited should know some time in advance of the coming of white people, so that the lamas may perform incantations and nullify the effect of possible evil influences.

As early as 1932 my decision to travel in disguise in Tibet was taken. I knew that if I avoided the districts usually visited by white people I had at least a slight chance to avoid being found out. The masses of the people in Tibet cannot read and their ideas about the appearance of white people are vague. To make things easier, Tibetan clothes are wide and loose, and completely hide the form of the body and the somewhat un-Tibetan gait of a white person. As a matter of fact, Tibetan clothes are so loose that on cold nights many Tibetans carry about a burning stove hidden in the folds of their garments. Sometimes a fairly good-sized dog may be transported in the same way.

The ignorance of the Tibetans about things and people outside Tibet is appalling and greatly facilitates travel in disguise. The most extraordinary ideas prevail about other parts of the world.

Tibetan brigands with whom I had the amusing adventures recorded in Chapter III thought that white people carried about foodstuffs inside their heads.

Tibetan nomads in whose tents I lived for a

day or so believed that Japan was an integral part of China and that Russia and America were more or less the same thing.

Only when in the neighbourhood of priests and monks I had to be on my guard. My only chance then was to pose as a deaf and dumb person.

Long before leaving for Asia I had realized the necessity of acquiring an immense resistance and staying-power for my travels in Tibet. I had to traverse the district south from Keria, where not a single blade of grass grows over a distance of several hundred miles. Animals would not be of the slightest use there, since they would die on the way from lack of food. I was determined to penetrate into a part of the world where the explorer is faced with that greatest and seemingly most insuperable of difficulties: the impossibility of taking beasts of burden for transport purposes. So I had to use another method, precisely the same as that which I recently used for traversing the bleak lava region of the Odadahraun in the uninhabited interior of Iceland, namely, that of carrying my food and equipment myself.

Travelling unaccompanied by beasts of burden involved a hitherto unknown simplification of equipment and the cutting down of seemingly indispensable utensils and food reserves to an absolute minimum. To give an example: the food, warm clothing, camp, and other equipment carried by the Haardt Expedition for every white person in the expedition for a period of forty-five days weighed one thousand pounds per head! The maximum I could carry when travelling unaccompanied by beasts of burden was about one-fifteenth of that quantity!

So I knew that in order to succeed I had to go into training to cover enormous distances on foot very quickly so that a comparatively small supply of food taken along should last over a distance of many hundred miles. Furthermore, I had to reduce greatly the amount of food taken and to get used to living on uncooked food of the simplest kind to save the weight of cooking-utensils.

Moreover, I realized that if I could sleep in an unheated tent at a temperature many degrees under freezing-point I could keep away from Tibetan tents and Tibetan houses whenever I chose—even during those terribly cold Tibetan nights—thus minimizing the chances of detection; and living on uncooked food would also give me the advantage of being able to hide myself much more easily. There is nothing more dangerous for the solitary traveller than the lighting of a fire. Even if nothing worse happens, it may signal his presence to the many bandits who infest Central Asia, where robbery is considered a respectable side-line.

As soon as my decision to travel in disguise in Tibet had been taken I went into training. In the autumn of 1933 I twice covered a distance of 80 miles in 24 hours each. Late in the autumn I began to walk longer distances at an *average* speed of 35 miles a day. One of these training-trips was a walk from Malmö in the south of Sweden to Stockholm, a distance of about 400 English miles covered in less than 12 days, fully packed. The latter performance attracted the attention of the Swedish press, my photograph appearing in the first page of *Dagens Nyheter*, one of the largest Stockholm dailies, on November 3, 1933. Few people who read the long newspaper reports in which I was compared with Gandhi, on account of my frugal habits, realized that the performance was really part of training for a journey to uninhabited and inaccessible parts of Central Asia.

Later in the year I spent many nights in an unheated tent in Northern Scandinavia at a temperature of many degrees under freezing-point, and lived for many weeks on uncooked food of the simplest kind without taking any stimulants. One morning when I crawled out from the tent the temperature was 5° Fahrenheit, so the prospect of Tibetan nights had lost its terror.

Soon afterwards I began to look out for suitable companions to accompany me to Central Asia. It sounds incredible that in a world where millions of people find time hanging heavily on their hands, it should have been impossible to find suitable companions for such an adventure. The few candidates who were up to my conditions physically, could not speak the many languages required for the journey or lacked the psychical and ethical qualifications necessary for successfully entering Tibet in disguise.

Later on, the news that I intended to travel in Asia leaked out and I realized the impossibility of keeping my plans secret any longer. When I found the news had leaked out anyhow, I had no objection to its finding its way into the newspapers, as I hoped that publicity would help me to find suitable companions by enabling me to get in touch with a very large number of candidates, from whom I could make my selection.

The *Sunday Express* was the first London paper to take an interest in the matter. Three articles were published about my expedition, the *Sunday Express* mentioning the fact that I was looking for companions to accompany me to Central Asia. The first article brought in hundreds of applications, many of them quite serious. Some applicants obviously exaggerated. One man wrote that he could walk 120 miles a day, but when I wrote him offering to put him to a test he did not feel inclined to carry on further correspondence regarding the matter.

Other applicants really meant business. A boy of nineteen actually cycled up non-stop from Liverpool to London, in order to show me his powers of resistance. Unfortunately, before he was put to the final tests, someone in his family was taken seriously ill, forcing him to give up the plan of coming along.

There were also lady applicants. One of them was particularly tenacious. She meant to "take good care of me and all the other members of the expedition" in Asia, and as I was not inhuman enough to put a woman to walking-tests of sixty English miles a day while depriving her of all possibilities of taking her usual tonics (I even banned tea during tests!), I had to turn her application down right in the beginning. The good lady then came to my house every ten minutes from morning till night, until everybody in the house was on the verge of hysteria.

Before they were actually put to the most trying tests, few applicants realized what it means to travel in the most inaccessible parts of Central Asia without the technical facilities and convenience usually considered indispensable for such a journey.

From end to end, the expedition was based

on simplification rather than complication. Tibetan yaks, for instance, travel at an average speed of only two miles an hour, and several hours are lost every morning in packing them. If one has no beasts of burden at all, one is ready in the morning in a few minutes, and then one starts at a speed of four and a half miles an hour. This method of travel is just as simple as it is efficient. I have used it not only in Tibet, but also in the uninhabited interior of Iceland, where I averaged daily walks of thirty-five miles.

My equipment included a very small and light device enabling me to cross rivers and lakes in any direction without attracting attention. The Empire News Reel filmed me with the device for the weekly news in the English cinemas, and maybe some of my readers remember having seen me on the news-reel. The film was taken at Finchley Open Air Swimming Pool, in the presence of some of the local authorities, and representatives of the local press. There were some funny accidents. Two different types of apparatus were tested and there were even spills, exciting spills, with people fully clothed falling into the water.

When travelling in Asia, the device was hidden in a bag made of sheepskin. It often proved to be very useful. Only in a high wind it became very dangerous, as it easily got out of control.

Just imagine a powerful blast of wind acting on the side of a floating device, having a surface of something like twenty square feet, but weighing only a few pounds! In a high wind it often whirled along like a dry leaf in the autumn. I remember crossing a lake in the boat with a strong wind blowing from behind, when the average speed worked out at more than fifteen miles an hour! When the wind blew in the opposite direction, the boat of course could not be used.

For crossing swift-flowing rivers I had provided it with two very small and light self-invented anchors which were thrown out alternately. As the Tibetan brigands thought that my anchors were some mysterious device for hooking ghosts they did not destroy them, nor did they dare to take them away, most Tibetans having a vague horror of "magical implements" which they fail to understand.

On the whole, however, these anchors were not quite so indispensable in Tibet as during my recent expedition to the uninhabited interior of Iceland.

My tent hardly weighed more than two pounds. It was such that I could look out from it in all directions, but it was not transparent when looked at from outside. Moreover, it was in two different colours—one inside and another outside—

permitting me to adapt myself to two different types of soil. The tent was extraordinarily light and yet so strong that even bad Tibetan storms could not undo it, provided, of course, that I succeeded in keeping the wind entirely out. Once the wind gets inside a tent, an infinitely smaller force is sufficient to tear it to pieces. On at least two occasions when bandits approached in the daytime, I quickly dug up the little tent to avoid confiscation. I was never attacked by bandits at night, as I invariably waited until total darkness had set in before putting up my tent. At the latitude of Tibet, night falls very rapidly, and daylight comes on very quickly in the morning. A few minutes before sunrise I would be on my way again.

One of my cameras was so small that it could go inside a match-box. I also had a lasso, a compass, a little pocket-lamp with a strong red light, and small field-glasses, which, by the way, were destroyed by robbers the very first time I happened to meet any. Many things which usually are considered indispensable for such a journey, such as cooking-apparatus, much spare linen, etc., were ruthlessly eliminated, as the saving of every ounce of weight was of paramount importance.

And how about weapons? I had . . . none at all!

Before leaving London, I consulted "Kim" on the matter. "Kim" happened to be in London, to which he had come from his house at Mayavati, near Pithoragarh, right near the border of Tibet. He advised me not to take any firearms at all—*provided I was not afraid.* "But if you are afraid," he added, "several machine-guns would not be enough!"

My simple ways of living, of course, greatly facilitated the journey. I am a non-smoker. I only smoke in the company of people who consider non-smoking a virtue. Also I do not drink or take tonics of any kind.

Had I been a smoker I should never have been able to carry out my plan to travel in Tibet in the disguise of a native. I should have had to load myself up with a large amount of tobacco on an expedition in which every ounce of additional weight diminished the chances of success.

Furthermore, the Tibetans are non-smokers, apart from a few *outré* individuals in the cities, where, by the way, it is forbidden to smoke. It is highly probable, therefore, that the odour of tobacco would have betrayed me again and again, not to speak of the additional inconvenience of signalling my presence to bandits by night, when lighting a pipe or cigarette. True, as a rule, Tibetan robbers are charming fellows and never hurt one (at least as far as Western

Tibet is concerned), but they often behave like curious children who destroy "toys" which they do not thoroughly understand. While systematically searching the belongings of the unprotected traveller they have a tendency to destroy things which sometimes are badly missed afterwards. So the more infrequently one meets with them the better.

For the same reason I never cooked food nor lit a fire to warm myself in Tibet, although dried dung was very abundant at times and could easily have been collected for this purpose.

The most carefully hidden part of my equipment was a small bottle containing the colour destined for dyeing my face and hands : a mixture of tincture of iodine and oil. Had this bottle been found by brigands searching me it would have meant the untimely end of the Tibetan adventure. However, the precious bottle was tucked away so securely that on one occasion the bandits who even found my camera, which was not larger than a match-box, failed to find the bottle. As the secret of its hiding-place might still be useful to me some day, I wish to hold it back, but I would like to add that its real efficacy rested on its extraordinary simplicity.

Long before leaving for Tibet, I took up the study of the language. It looks terribly complicated and there are different vocabularies and styles of address according to the rank of the person addressed. Since I had made up my mind to speak Tibetan only when mixing with the ordinary people, I of course laid the greatest stress on the expressions to be used in addressing humble folk, and this somewhat facilitated matters. However, as I was out to listen to educated people as well, I had to carry my theoretical studies of Tibetan a step farther.

Although, on the whole, Tibetan is very different from Japanese, the fact that I had formerly studied the latter greatly facilitated the study of Tibetan on account of many structural and fundamental similarities. Polite prefixes, for instance, exist in both languages. In many cases you need not say "mine" or "yours". If you say "the stupid wife", everybody will understand that you mean your *own* wife.

Even the common vocabulary may often be similar in both languages. Tea, for instance, is translated *tsha* or *otsha* in Japanese. In Tibetan, tea is called *ja* (the "j" pronounced as in French). One, two, three, four are translated *ichi, ni, san, shi* in Japanese, and *tshig, nji, sum, ji* (like "j" in *jamais*) in Tibetan. Even the knowledge of a little Turkish helps one in learning Tibetan. "Water", for instance, is translated *su*, in Turkish. In Tibetan, it is *tshu*.

The Tibetan language is as rich in flowery

expressions as other Oriental languages. Just as you say "a man having a long posterior" in Japanese for "a man who likes to remain seated a long time", you say "the snapping of one's fingers" in Tibetan for "a moment", or "he has a long tail" for "he is steadfast in friendship".

Moreover, in Tibetan it is possible to convey various grades of politeness by altering one's speech, the shortest expression usually being the least polite one, just as in English "shut up" is much less polite than "would you do me the favour to stop talking".

The author has had considerable practical experience in the linguistic field. In Europe I have spoken about ten different languages before the various microphones of broadcasting stations in different countries, but I never studied a more interesting language than Tibetan.

Since I intended to travel via Turkistan, I advised the Russian Embassy in London of my intention to do so, and soon afterwards applied to the Russian Government in Moscow for permission to travel across Russia. After lengthy consideration the Russian Foreign Office refused permission. I certainly had not expected such a decision, all the more so since all the other governments with whom I had come into contact had proven most friendly and obliging. Had I anticipated a refusal by the Moscow Government, I certainly should not have approached them at all, but would have taken up negotiations direct with the Government of the Kirghiz Republic in Frunze or Pishpek. But once the Central Government had issued their veto, it was too late to approach the local government, and the only course open was to defy the Russian Government, relying on the valuable assistance of three powerful Kirghiz chiefs, whose names I do not mention for obvious reasons. Should the political situation in Turkistan undergo a radical change in the future, I shall write another book on my adventures and experiences in Turkistan. In 1934 the limit of the Russian zone of influence in Turkistan was about half-way between Jarkand and Chotan.

During the first few years following the Great War there were no relations whatsoever between Soviet Russia and Chinese Turkistan. The local Soviet Government in Tashkent and the Sinkiang Government simply ignored each other, and the frontier was closed. However, the presence of many Russian refugees in Eastern Turkistan who might have organized a *coup* against the Reds from across the border, irritated the Soviets and they finally extended certain trade facilities to the Sinkiang Government in exchange for a promise given by the latter to "invite" Russian refugees to return to Soviet Russia.

An amnesty was promised to the poor devils, although no one seemed to be able to tell me whether, and to what extent, the promise was kept.

This agreement, concluded a few years after the Great War, was the first step towards Russian penetration into Chinese Turkistan. This penetration was both economic and political. It was greatly assisted by an elaborate system of bribing. It has gone on ever since, and became more evident as the years went by.

During the revolt of the population against the Urumtshi Government in 1931, 1932, and 1933, things were ripe for open "co-operation" between the Sinkiang Government and Soviet Russia. A Russian army—although not nominally Russian, but yet Russian in fact—came in disguise over the frontier to fight the insurrection of the popular General Ma against the Sinkiang Government.

Today, Ma, the popular General Ma, has mysteriously disappeared. It seems that he has been kept prisoner somewhere in Russia, if nothing worse has happened to him.

At the time when I visited Chinese Turkistan, open fighting had ceased, but underground strife by intrigues and bribes still went on. The mighty underground opponent of Soviet Russia in that part of the world, is not, as many people erroneously imagine, the British Empire, but *Japan*.

When I was half-way from Jarkand to Chotan I was no longer in danger from the Russians, and brigands prying on unprotected travellers became the chief danger.

Since even a well-trained and highly resistant body cannot for very long stand the strain of average walks of thirty-five English miles a day whilst living mostly on uncooked barley meal, the Tibetan journey had to be effected during the most favourable season of one year while the mountains in Northern and Central Tibet are free from snow up to an altitude of 16,500 feet. A considerable portion of this best period of the year coincides with the rainy season, a very lucky circumstance, since it would have been impossible for me to carry water over a distance of several hundred miles in addition to my equipment and the scanty amount of food necessary for such a long trip across uninhabited areas.

Every minute saved was of the greatest importance. Apart from ensuring a greater secrecy regarding my movements in inhabited or bandit-infested territories, my being able to live on uncooked food during very long periods also saved an enormous amount of valuable time in uninhabited areas. At altitudes between 12,000 and 15,000 feet water begins to boil at a temperature as low as about 65° Centigrade, with the result that food boils in water of low temperature and takes perhaps five or six times longer to get ready than food cooked at sea level.

Only once was I actually on the verge of starvation. The white intruder travelling in Tibet in disguise cannot take along bulky and weighty apparatus destined to locate his exact bearings. He is therefore exposed to the serious danger of making geographical mistakes. On one occasion, owing to such a mistake in locating the nearest inhabited place, my food supply ran out, and I had nothing to eat for more than three days. The white desert seemed endless, and not even a blade of grass was visible. Even grass would have been a godsend to me, since I happen to be a vegetarian!

I coolly weighed the awkward situation. Another two days' walk to the nearest district where I could obtain food and no prospect of finding anything to eat anywhere! Fortunately, it happened to be the rainy season and I had at least as much water as I wanted. I carefully examined my equipment. I *had* to eat up something.

I then remembered that in former times some of the Indian tribes in America had lived on bark. There were neither trees nor even shrubs in that part of Tibet, but a small portion of my equipment was made of wood. So I chipped off a piece, washed it several times, ground it into sawdust, and swallowed it. It tasted horrible, but since sawdust contains at least ten per cent of oil, it kept me going.

I jokingly mentioned this incident during an interview I gave to a large Stockholm paper in 1935. It published a fine cartoon showing me taking a "sawdust lunch". I hope the paper did not get into trouble with its friends in the foodstuff industry, who cannot possibly like a newspaper giving away to the public dangerous secrets, the publication of which might prove detrimental to the interests of the foodstuff industry.

Apart from "sawdust lunches" the white desert was not so terrible after all. Although I was quite alone for about two weeks without seeing a human being, solitude did not upset me very much, especially not the lone solitudes of mysterious Tibet where one finds oneself.

Only when nothing whatsoever goes on *within* ourselves, the absence of outer sensations becomes unbearable.

Even such seemingly unpleasant experiences as crossing endless uninhabited areas without any vegetation may be interesting and a welcome change. When viewed in the right way the most arid places have a peculiar charm of their own. The variety of colour in some of the deserts in Tibet is sometimes exquisite, and those of my readers who have travelled in the uninhabited interior of Iceland will know how beautiful such desolate places can be.

Tibet is profoundly quiet. Having lived in the Arctic regions I, for one, do know what profound silence means, and yet Tibetan silence is deeper still. Only when the wind begins to blow, which usually occurs in the afternoons, there comes a strange concert of awe-inspiring, discordant tones, like the roar of thousands of evil spirits.

Especially the great northern tableland in Tibet has a terrible climate. The nights are bitterly cold all the year round, but the afternoons in the summer are unpleasantly warm. Differences in temperature amounting to 60° Centigrade in a day very often occur. The tableland is swept by terrible winds, whirling up sand and salt crusts which penetrate into the nose, the mouth, and under the clothes. In no other part of the world has my resistance to cold and exposure and my considerable lung-capacity stood me in better stead than in Tibet.

Even in Western countries I only breathe about 3 times a minute, whereas most white people breathe not less than 15 times per minute, as they use only about one-tenth of their lung capacity for breathing. If someone who usually breathes 15 times a minute tried to walk in Tibet at an altitude of say, 13,000 feet, at a speed of 4½ miles an hour, he would soon breathe 3 times per *second* and most certainly have a breakdown after covering a few hundred yards.

Let me add a warning here.

My slow rhythm of breathing *is not the result of breathing exercises*. One should never try to change the rhythm of breathing by conscious action. If one makes a conscious effort to breathe slowly because air costs nothing and one expects to gain something by slow breathing—no matter whether the advantage in view is spiritual or material—*one sooner or later destroys oneself by the exercises*. In most cases conscious breathing practised for the purpose of getting something leads to nervous breakdowns if not to something worse.

Breathing should be unconscious. If we change from *within*, if we treat everything outside ourselves in the same way as we wish to be treated by others, we cease to be in the state of virtual cramp which causes incomplete breathing. If we voluntarily draw a limit to our egotism and only take from life as much as we need to maintain life and not more, we cease to be in this state of cramp, psychically and physically.

In a relaxed body, deep and slow breathing sets in *automatically and unconsciously*. But if one tries to bring about slow breathing *by conscious action* without first changing the fundamental cause of wrong breathing, viz. egocentricism, one is on the road to utter destruction.

This warning seems to be necessary as hundreds of people both in Tibet and in the Occident have become nervous wrecks or lunatics by conscious breathing exercises.

Is it not strange that the most valuable equipment for a journey to Tibet—right breathing—cannot be bought for money, nor can it be acquired by any outward practices without leading to self-destruction? And is it not strange that at a time when aeroplanes fly across the Atlantic, the most secret parts of Tibet should remain inaccessible to anyone attempting to force open the door to her secrets in a conquering spirit?

Once a person has simplified matters and is not afraid of anything it is really not so very difficult to travel in disguise and face occasional hardships and privations. So-called "big" things are not so immeasurably difficult to carry out. It is really easier to travel some time under the most difficult conditions than it is to live only a few months with a woman one dislikes. The small problems of everyday life are often just as hard to solve satisfactorily as apparently enormous propositions.

And then do dangers and privations really matter if every day brings a fresh and novel experience? Moreover, dangers and difficulties lose their significance altogether if at heart we are not afraid. One can turn anthills into mountains, but also vice versa.

The worse dangers are, of course, the unexpected ones.

One night, soon after having fallen asleep, I awoke feeling terribly exhausted. My whole body was covered with murderous leeches which sucked the blood out through my clothes. Their bite was not painful and I might have bled to death had I not noticed the creatures in time. The leeches were a danger, but taking all in all they were not much worse than some of the subtle poisons of civilization which may take years to take effect but get their man just as surely as the Tibetan leeches, unless their victim realizes the danger in time.

Apart from leeches and animals of a parasitic nature, I seldom had trouble with so-called wild animals, which, by the way, are not nearly so wild in Tibet as animals of the same kinds in other parts of the world, since they are never hunted by the Tibetans. Near the border of the white desert I awoke in the morning to find the tent surrounded by animals staring curiously at that strange and helpless creature needing such an unnatural and clumsy thing as a tent to protect himself on the storm-bitten plateau of Northern Tibet, on which no human being has ever dared to settle. It was obvious that many of the animals I met had never seen a human being before. Wild yaks came quite near without showing any signs of fear or discomfort. They were just curious and gave a good stare. Birds, which are usually very shy in the West, strutted about like barnyard fowls while I folded my tent in the morning.

I often wondered how my friends the animals faced those terrible rainfalls in Northern Tibet, which sometimes literally sweep away everything. Rain may come down in enormous quantities, and there being no possibility of rapid drainage in most parts of Tibet, apart from the permanently flowing rivers in the south, whole Tibetan landscapes may be rapidly turned into lakes after a torrential rainfall, and wide and swollen rivers occasionally appear in districts where, normally, even small streamlets are non-existent. What a thrill to cross such rivers in a light floating-device hidden in a bag made of sheepskin, throwing out alternately two small anchors! Sometimes those swift-flowing and powerful one-or-two-day rivers suddenly disappear in the ground. A few minutes after such a rainfall the air again becomes as clear as crystal and mountains which are a hundred miles distant seem to be so near that one feels tempted to touch them by hand.

CHAPTER II

AMONGST KIND AND HOSPITABLE TIBETAN NOMADS

I HAD not been in Asia for something like thirteen years, and eagerly anticipated meeting my first Tibetans.

Here they were, looking rather filthy, but happy and peaceable. They wore very full gowns with almost ridiculously long sleeves, reminding one of a small boy wearing the jacket of his father. Their boots were made of felt and rose just above the knee with a slit behind the knee. One of the men standing in the group seemed to be a little more prosperous than the others, for his hair was adorned with numerous rings made of ivory.

Yaks and sheep were with them as beasts of burden. One hardly believes one's eyes in Tibet when looking at a sheep fully loaded up by the Tibetans. The load seems to be quite out of proportion to the size and strength of the poor little animal. But people all over the Orient are wont to put domestic animals to exceedingly hard work. This tendency is manifest all over the East. In the Balkans you may often see a fat and majestic native weighing at least fifteen stone comfortably seated on the back of a poor frail little donkey which almost disappears under his bulky body.

Domestic animals seem to be the only creatures which are not treated very kindly in Tibet. Wild animals and even lice receive very gentle treatment.

Particularly in the north and the centre of the country the Tibetans are very muscular and broad-shouldered but rather short. Only later on in the south I met some very tall people. The Tibetans are very gay in spite of their dreary surroundings. They are fond of music and play queerly on cymbals and trumpets in a manner which seems to be rather monotonous to Western ears.

The herdsmen, obviously, were not used to meeting strangers. They were greatly frightened when I approached, and some of them actually took to their heels. When people appear in groups, the herdsmen become frightened immediately, for the strangers may be brigands. But when a stranger comes along all alone, it may be worse. He may be a—ghost.

Our first conversation confirmed their fear of ghosts. They asked me whether I had met anyone. "Yes," I replied quietly, "I met a bear yesterday afternoon."

"A bear!" they exclaimed. "Did he speak to you?"

"No," I said, astonished. "He did not."

They seemed greatly relieved. It was a good thing that I was no ghost, and the fact that I had not had contacts with ghosts quite recently made matters still easier.

The herdsmen of Northern Tibet regard the bear with dread, although he very seldom attacks anybody. They say that bears are manifestations of evil spirits, and even in cases where they are not ghosts they are not bears but *men*, descendants of primitive men that have lost the faculty of speech.

The herdsman who looked most prosperous—the one with the ivory rings in his hair—offered me hospitality. He uttered his invitation in a very kind and soft voice. Nearly all Tibetan herdsmen speak softly and much less hurriedly than we do in Western countries.

None of these herdsmen had ever seen a white person and the possibilities of detection were slight.

Only my face, hands, and scalp were dyed. My supply of colour—a mixture of iodine and oil—was strictly limited. Moreover, although iodine partly evaporates when rubbed into the skin, a portion of it is absorbed by the body, which would cause poisoning if iodine was used in large quantities and the whole body was treated with it. A person suffering from iodine poisoning, be it ever so slight, could not walk up to forty miles a day.

Great as these distances seem to be to white people, they are well within the physical possibilities of most Tibetans, who often walk thirty miles and more in a single day, sometimes without stopping to eat. In a country where no wheeled conveyances exist and all travel is effected on horseback or on foot, people naturally get used to walking enormous distances.

My host took me to his tent. There was only one "room" in it. It was very large and exhaled a terrible odour of dung, decayed meat, and rancid butter mingled with the smell of a variety of human refuse.

My host's wife seemed very much at ease, a strange thing in Asia. Women in Tibet are considered equal to men and they are never treated in the humiliating fashion tolerated by the feminine sex in Turkistan or in India. Tibetan women feel themselves equal to men and are quite at ease in their presence. Only in strictly religious matters there seems to be a slight discrimination against women. The highest benediction of the lamas, viz. tickling the crown of the head with a kind of tassel, is reserved for men. Women cannot get this blessing, even against payment of a high fee.

My host never showed the slightest interest in his children. He did not seem to care for them more than he cared for his felt shoes. But my hostess was exceedingly kind to them. This seems to be a general practice all over Tibet. Only mothers show love and kindness towards their children, fathers being quite indifferent.

The Tibetans chatter a good deal. They put just as many superfluous and inessential questions as many Westerners, but I must add that although they talk greatly they never gossip unkindly about other people behind their backs.

The Tibetans are perhaps the kindest of all the peoples of Asia. Before meeting some of the lamas of the worst type I never saw a single instance of brutality, falsehood, or dishonesty. Not even Tibetan brigands were really brutal when robbing me.

However, idle curiosity seems to be rife. Whenever a stranger appears he is subjected to a flood of questions. "*Kyod gana yon?*" "*Kyod tshi la yon?*" "*Kyod su in?*"—Where do you come from? Why do you come? Who are you? etc. You hear these questions wherever you go. When travelling in disguise it is of course necessary to take the precaution to avoid people or tents after crossing wide uninhabited areas, until one has reached places situated a little beyond the districts bordering on uninhabited territories.

Occasionally the rapid changes in temperature nearly got me into serious trouble. My face, hands, and scalp were subject to those sudden fluctuations in temperature amounting from thirty to fifty degrees, which are not infrequent in Tibet, and since such sudden changes may make the skin crack at any time they were to me a very real danger. Often the faulty spots had to be repainted immediately, but it was sometimes difficult to find some satisfactory excuse for withdrawing immediately to repaint my face and hands.

After our evening meal, consisting of barley meal mixed with buttered tea, meat, and cheese, the family stayed inside their tent. The smell was terrible, but the Tibetans are inured to it. It's a matter of fact, the farther East one travels the less the sense of smell of people seems to be developed.

My host told a few jokes, the point of which I failed to see. Perhaps one needs long training to see the point of Tibetan jokes. He then went on to narrate a pious legend he had heard from a travelling lama. I gathered that it was about a holy man, so holy that he gave away everything : all his money he gave away to the poor; his eyes he gave to the blind ; and his wife to someone who wanted her. How very touching ! Tibetan legends never glorify strength and power as most Western legends do. They glorify renunciation and deeds of kindness.

The family then "went to bed". The Tibetan nomads sleep naked in their tents. I, of course, could not do likewise.

Before falling asleep I congratulated myself on having succeeded in keeping out of trouble. Things had gone better than I had expected. On the whole it had been very easy to hide the fact that I was not a Tibetan. The family had not had the faintest suspicion that I was no Tibetan.

I had talked, of course, as little as possible, and about very simple things only, listening dreamily to everything of interest they had to say. Whenever there was a possibility of my getting into trouble by not being able to understand exactly what they had said, I had a "fit of holiness" and retired to pray.

They probably took me for a very strange Tibetan from a distant corner of Tibet who was rather stupid and shy, and had occasional fits of craziness, but, nevertheless, at all times they were friendly, hospitable, and considerate.

The next morning I had to run away soon after sunrise.

The Tibetans are very fond of decayed meat with worms in it. As meat keeps fresh almost indefinitely in Tibet, they must go to a lot of trouble to get their favourite delicacy. They mix the various organs taken from the body of a slaughtered animal and keep the mixture at a fairly high temperature for several days. The mixture is buried in the ground, and dug out a fortnight later. It is then filled into small delicacy bags which roughly correspond to the chocolate boxes of young ladies in the West.

Late in the evening the family had transported their belongings into the tent. The temperature was about freezing-point outside and the delicacy bag was frozen. It began to melt soon after sunrise and the smell was such that I had to make a dash for fresh air.

My host looked very surprised. It was probably the first time in his life that he had seen a human being inconvenienced by this *delicious odour*. He probably thought I was fastidious.

In some districts of Tibet it is a pleasant pastime of the Tibetans to gather for eating-matches. Large quantities of the cheapest kind of food available, usually barley-meal, are eaten, and he who manages to eat the largest quantity is proclaimed the winner. The rules regarding the game are very strict and if one of the participants retires during the match, be it only for a few seconds, he is instantly disqualified. In some districts the population takes some interest in these contests, but I never saw any really wise Tibetans who are capable of independent thinking ever present at one.

Some of the participants go into training a few days or weeks before the event by taking food enough for at least four or five men. They fast only immediately before the match.

Sports in a Western sense are practically unknown in most parts of Tibet. Walking at high speeds, however, and running and skating are practised. Tibetan skates are made of bone, and not metal.

I failed to ascertain exactly the quantity eaten by the winner of such a Tibetan eating-contest, but another nomad family with whom I stayed two days later assured me that one of their friends had eaten like between ten and fourteen pounds at one sitting.

In the presence of my hosts and a few friends, a Tibetan told a joke he had heard about overeating.

A Tibetan going about quite alone suddenly met a gigantic snake of awe-inspiring appearance, of a kind he had never seen nor heard of before. He took to his heels and from a hiding-place tremblingly watched the apparition.

The snake attacked various small animals and

devoured them with great voraciousness. As the animal went on eating for hours, it grew bigger and bigger until its skin was extended almost to bursting-point.

At that moment the snake gave a loud hiss and a magician came out of his den and handed to it a little red ball. Hardly had the snake swallowed the ball, when it began to shrink. Its body almost instantly ceased to be dilated, and assumed normal proportions.

The magician left a few of his red balls on the ground and the snake started again to devour all the little animals it could get hold of, gradually moving away from the place where the Tibetan was in hiding.

"How interesting!" thought the Tibetan. "If I could get hold of one of those little red balls, I could take it at an eating-match after having eaten my fill, and then go on eating, thus winning the contest."

When the snake had moved away sufficiently, he quickly ran forward, picked up one of the little red balls and ran home with it as fast as he could.

A few days later he hid the ball in his *amfrag* (breast-pocket) while he took part in an eating-contest. After having stuffed himself to bursting-point with the contents of thirty bowls of *tsamba* (barley-meal), he stealthily took out the ball from his breast-pocket and swallowed it.

Suddenly his body began to melt down, and it disappeared before the eyes of the astonished audience.

Only the thirty bowls of *tsamba* (barley-meal), which he had eaten, remained, dressed up in Tibetan clothes. For the red balls of the magician possessed the magical power to dissolve organic matter, with the remarkable exception of snake's flesh!

After hearing this joke the Tibetan nomads remained silent for a few seconds, and then there came a lusty roar of merriment lasting perhaps a whole minute. The Tibetans are extraordinarily gay people, and have a good laugh whenever they hear a joke or see something unusual. I think if something had turned up to lay bare my disguise, making me suddenly appear before them as a white person, their first reaction would have been boundless merriment at so unfamiliar a sight.

With such primitive people the chances of being found out, however, are naturally small. The next day was the fifth I spent in the company of these Tibetan nomads. On this day a little colour went off my hair and I stood there with a streak of fair hair. This is probably about the worst thing which may happen to a man travelling in disguise. I had not noticed it myself until my attention was drawn to it by some of the nomads calmly discussing the strange fact that so young a man should already have a streak of *white* hair!

The next day, however, a much more serious thing happened, which forced me to leave the district in a hurry.

After partaking of one of the Tibetan meals, which invariably consist of barley-meal, buttered tea, cheese and meat (I usually refused the latter), I felt the need to take a little bicarbonate. (My travelling pharmacy consisted of a small packet of bicarbonate to counteract the effects of bad food and a little radio-active earth for disinfecting water.)

I stealthily added a tiny pinch of bicarbonate to the buttered tea. No one had noticed it.

When I stirred the liquid with the fingers, as Tibetan etiquette demands, a number of bubbles formed, and the tepid mixture looked as if it was seething. My Tibetan friends appeared greatly frightened. When I put the bowl to my lips there were cries of horror, but I gulped down the liquid before they could snatch it from me.

They all stood round me petrified with horror.

I felt rather uncomfortable over this fuss about such a simple thing. I failed to understand why on earth they were so terrified. Why did they stare at me like that without saying a word? Had I been found out? Had they suddenly discovered that I was one of those *pee-lins* (white persons) concerning whom they had heard so many nasty things from the priests?

Should I try to escape?

Many thoughts crossed my mind while they stared at me aghast for a few minutes without a word. After a little while one of them touched my hand and said tremblingly: *"Shi ma zin."* (He is not dead yet.)

"No, he is not dead. It is a miracle!" echoed the others.

"I am glad he is not dead," joyously cried a young Tibetan girl who, during my short stay with the family, had showered on me many marks of interest.

I stood up.

"And he is not even ill!" exclaimed a Tibetan boy.

"He takes poison and it has no effect on him!" cried another.

Had somebody tried to poison me then? I endeavoured to elucidate the mystery. But all their former familiarity with me was gone now. They regarded me as a saint who could swallow poison with impunity.

It was some days before I found an explanation of what had happened. To Tibetan eyes, the fizzing of a tepid liquid is conclusive proof that the liquid contains poison. When I had added bicarbonate of soda to the buttered tea big bubbles were formed in the liquid, and my Tibetan friends had stared at me aghast while I drank the "poison" because they had expected me to fall down stone dead.

This unfortunate incident destroyed the familiarity with which I had been treated by them till then. I became a "great saint" and the rumour of the "miracle" began to spread. It was the wisest course for me to disappear from the district as quickly as possible, before the news of the "miracle" reached the lamas, which would, no doubt, have led to an inquiry and a thorough examination of the "holy man".

When I came to the tents of other Tibetan nomads four or five days later I had covered a distance of about 190 miles in four days, although the straight line between the two places was hardly more than 80 or 90.

Four naked Tibetan ladies were seated in the tent and did not seem embarrassed in any way, nor did they make the slightest attempt to cover themselves or dress when a stranger entered.

Ordinarily, Tibetan women do not seem to know what shame means. They are not afraid to show themselves as God made them. I have found some exceptions to this rule, however, in the case of expectant mothers. All those who have travelled in countries where women show themselves *au naturel*, will know that only expectant mothers hide their bodies.

It seems as though Nature herself had given expectant mothers an instinctive desire to hide in order to prevent sexual intercourse during that period. If anything may be called unnatural, sexual intercourse with pregnant women deserves that name. Tibetan occultists of the advanced type say that it is a veritable crime against the child to come and against humanity.

They also say that sexual intercourse with expectant mothers is the real and primary cause of cancer. It creates a latent disposition to cancer in the man, the woman, and the child. Tibetan occultists are, of course, unable to prove this scientifically.

Cases of cancer do occur in Tibet, but it seems to be much rarer there than in Western countries, where cancer mortality increases from year to year to an alarming degree in spite of hundreds of millions spent on cancer research and the anti-cancer campaign.

Tibetan women do not wash, whatever the circumstances. A male Tibetan who washes his body with water would be despised as a weakling, but a Tibetan woman using water for cleaning her body would "wash her happiness away", which is much more serious. Usually the body is cleaned with butter or mustard and utensils with sand.

The Tibetan nomads do not work much, but they are nevertheless occupied practically all day, since they do everything in very leisurely fashion. They would drive to despair most of our Western efficiency experts if they had a chance of studying them. "*Ka-le, ka-le*" (Go slow, go slow) is a standard expression with them.

To make butter, for instance, they put milk into bags made of sheepskin. The bags are rolled forward and backward for many hours, until butter is formed. Tibetan butter is incredibly cheap. Often twenty or forty pounds of butter are hardly sufficient to buy one pound of dried vegetables.

I always attracted rather embarrassing attention by my inability to consume enormous quantities of butter. The Tibetans take a great deal of butter and then often butter which is many months old. The more horrible it smells the more they seem to enjoy it. I once watched a Tibetan boy eat at least half a pound of rancid butter at a single meal.

The inhabited area drew nearer. There, greater precautions would have to be taken so that I should not be suspected. Nevertheless, I hoped that in view of the fact that the various parts of Tibet are very different in many respects, the masses of the people in the permanently inhabited part would consider my foreign accent and strange Tibetan syntax as being due to my hailing from some remote part of Tibet. As to learned people, priests, and monks, I had made up my mind not to speak to them at all and to pose as a deaf and dumb person and so avoid suspicion on the score of illiteracy.

With cordial shouts of *kale peb* (bon voyage) and *kale yuden jag* (good-bye, literally translated "please make yourself comfortable") I took leave of those nice Tibetan nomads whose kindness and simplicity had greatly impressed me.

CHAPTER III

ADVENTURES WITH BRIGANDS

THE Tibetan nomads are very leisurely people, but the Tibetan bandits are quick fellows, appearing and disappearing with lightning-like rapidity. The Tibetans call them *gyog-pas*, which is also the word for "quick" or "rapid".

Amongst my strange experiences in Tibet was the tactful warding-off of bandits.

Robbery is but seldom punished in Tibet. Bandits prey on unprotected travellers practically everywhere, but few of them are what may be called professional robbers. Most of them are merely people whose so-called honest businesses are suffering from temporary depression. If a Tibetan merchant goes bankrupt, for instance, he is not very much upset. It soon becomes known that he has simply become a bandit, and the moment he has robbed long enough to collect sufficient money to enable him again to take up his former honest profession, he will do so.

In most parts of Tibet the bandits are quite good-natured fellows. They never kill their victims unless the latter start the scrap by killing or wounding one of the members of the gang, and if the robbers are unpleasant in some cases this is due more to their ignorance and childlike curiosity than to actual malice.

On one occasion they cut out the lens of my film camera, filled it with water from a salt lake near by, and rinsed it thoroughly. They then fetched drinking-water, filled the camera with it, and tried to drink out of it. When they found that it was no good for any of the purposes which they could attribute to it, they put the lens back in its place and returned the camera to me with thanks.

They also took a delight in opening the films in broad daylight and playing with them like so many children enjoying a new toy they have never seen before.

Amongst my many encounters with the gentlemen of the Tibetan bandit profession, two were particularly eventful and amusing.

One day I came across a large gang of robbers numbering from twenty to thirty tough fellows, most of them wearing talismans round their necks. Talismans destined to bring luck to robbers are often specially consecrated and sold by the lamas.

The gang came on rather threateningly. Although they were probably quite good fellows at heart, they felt it necessary to give themselves

ADVENTURES WITH BRIGANDS 65

a warlike appearance in the interests of their profession. They probably thought that I should run away, or at least look terribly frightened.

My calm demeanour obviously embarrassed them. An aggressor whose victim does not defend himself, whilst showing no fear whatsoever so that it is quite obvious that fear is not the reason of his non-resistance, must always feel a little disarmed. He must vaguely feel that a greater force than mere brute resistance stands in the way of his aggression.

When they saw that I did not run away, the robbers hesitated a moment as if held back by some invisible barrier. Then a few of the more bellicose fellows, carried away by their business routine, stepped forward to search my belongings.

They were visibly taken aback when they found a pair of trousers, usually worn as an undergarment by Tantric priests, who are supposed to possess strong magical powers and to rule over many evil spirits.

They again hesitated a little, but finally their business routine got the better of them and they continued systematically to search my belongings.

The sight of a safety-pin greatly puzzled them.

"What is this?" they asked.

I held my tongue. How on earth could I briefly explain to Tibetan robbers the innumerable uses of this crowning glory of civilization, the safety-pin, a real godsend to the lonely traveller?

"I never saw such a thing before. It may be a magical instrument belonging to a mighty magician," observed one of the brigands.

Anything the Tibetans fail to understand is likely to be turned by them into a magical implement.

"It is perhaps used for hooking evil spirits," hazarded another.

"And the evil spirit may be there already, hooked," put in a third robber in a faltering voice.

Just as they reached my tent and were considering whether they should take it away, there was a sudden gust of wind. This was rather an unusual happening, since the wind seldom blows in the forenoon in Tibet. The blast was quite violent, and it was difficult to keep one's feet.

"Leave this magician alone," advised one of the gang.

"He will bring misfortune on us," observed another tough brigand. "He has mysterious implements"—meaning my safety-pins—"magicians' trousers, and keeps his eyes half closed."

I, of course, always kept my blue eyes half closed while I was in Tibet. I could have dyed them, but continual dyeing is harmful to the eyes.

"If he opens them fully, it may mean disaster," said another brigand in a low voice.

"There is something queer about this man," said a stately robber, probably the leader of the gang, who had quietly watched proceedings up to that moment, holding himself at a distance like a general conducting operations. "After all, he has nothing of value except a tent, a little food, a few coins, and some magical implements. Let us go."

And they all went on, not daring to look at me fully.

My next encounter with the gentlemen of the Tibetan brigand profession was perhaps even more amusing.

There were only six or seven of them. They were not mounted, and saw me in the evening coming along quite alone and unprotected. It was a very swampy district and the night falls rapidly at a latitude of 33 degrees. Putting to use my knowledge of swampy areas, I escaped, and the brigands spent a few hours roaming about and looking for the place where I was hiding. I had carefully chosen a fairly dry patch of ground, reached by a tortuous approach across a bad swamp, so that in the dark it was impossible for them to locate the place. After continuing their search for quite a long time, and after making sure that I had not left the neighbourhood, the robbers decided to wait until daybreak.

Continuing their search in the early morning, they located my tent just before sunrise, and one of the robbers, failing to follow my carefully selected tortuous approach to the dry patch of ground, made a short cut across the swampy ground and was pulled down up to his chest, within a distance of six or eight yards from my tent.

He shouted pitifully, while the swamp dragged him down inexorably. His comrades were too far behind to help him and the last thing in the world he expected was assistance from his prospective victim.

Then I threw out my lasso. The poor chap could hardly believe his eyes. A few seconds later he was on dry ground, looking rather helpless and not knowing what to do.

In Western countries the first idea after pulling a man out of a swamp is to make him dry his clothes. Such a thought never occurs to one in Tibet. Even when a Tibetan slips when fording a river in icily cold weather and gets drenched to the skin, he will go on walking in the bitter cold, or will calmly sit down as if nothing had happened.

The other brigands were still a hundred yards away and had seen the rescue of their comrade.

They still stood at a distance, doubting the evidence of their senses. After some hesitation they cautiously advanced.

A few moments later we were all seated on the ground in two circles. They cooked my breakfast together with their own and, wishing to make a special effort to express their gratitude, they added for me the choicest delicacy one can possibly obtain in Tibet, and which is eaten only on very rare occasions, viz: *sko-tse*, a mixture of leaves formed into balls and having a delicious taste when fried in butter.

"*Kyod gana yon?*"* was one of their first questions.

"From very far," I replied. "From the border of *Bod*."†

The brigands felt a little uneasy. The farther a man has travelled the more he is likely to be accompanied by *yi-dags* (ghosts). Had they known that I travel at least 10,000 miles every year, they might have jumped up and run away.

"You do not look and talk like a Tibetan," suddenly said one of the brigands, a very shrewd fellow who, I found later, apparently had travelled a good deal himself and had met many people.

---

* "Where do you come from?"
† Tibet.

His question caused the whole gang to look at me attentively.

"I have travelled very much," I responded. "And even in countries outside Tibet."

"Outside Tibet! Outside Tibet!" echoed the whole gang. It sounded almost as when white people might say, "He has been to the moon."

"I have travelled very much myself," declared the shrewd bandit, who had noticed that there was something un-Tibetan about me, "but I have never been outside Tibet."

"That must be a great adventure—to travel outside Tibet," observed another.

"Have you visited many countries?"

"Yes, I have."

"Have you ever been in the country of the *pee-lin*?"

"I have met white people," I answered evasively. I only told the truth when I said that.

"Is it true that they have barley-meal in their heads which shines out through their eyes, making their eyes look so colourless and ugly that *bod-pas** would be disgusted in their presence?"

"I never saw barley-meal in the heads of white people," I replied truthfully.

Two brigands had been talking together in

---
* Tibetans.

low tones. Obviously they put me down as a braggart who only boasted that he had met white people.

"If you have travelled so much," said the shrewd bandit, with a slight touch of suspicion in his voice, "you must have also met the people in India who have ears like deer."

"Have *you* seen them?" I asked.

"No," he answered; "but it is a well-known fact that people in India have ears like deer."

Being very anxious to confine the conversation to simple matters and to speak as little as possible myself, I changed the topic and, instead of ethnological problems, we soon talked about such simple matters as food, drink, the weather, and the life, in which my knowledge of colloquial Tibetan did not leave me in the lurch so often.

We later separated the best of friends.

"It is all very nice of you to tell us that you have met white people," observed one of the less polite bandits in parting, "but I don't believe a word of it." He was obviously no gentleman. He did not know the art of insulting people nicely.

To take away the sting of this unkind remark, another bandit added to the parting present a few feathers of the *kwa-ta*. These feathers are very useful. If you are taken ill you put them on your head and they will prevent your seeing ghosts.

Most Tibetans see ghosts everywhere. No house, no tent, not even the most barren desert, where no human being would ever dare to settle, is free from them. Ghosts may lurk in the dung left behind by the yaks or establish themselves comfortably in their cooking-utensils. Often the bandits themselves are mistaken for ghosts. It may happen that Tibetan nomads are robbed by bandits and after the departure of the brigands the victims may believe that the whole robbery has been an hallucination! It is not until they begin to miss the things taken away by the bandits that they become convinced of the reality of the apparition.

On the other hand, however, the Tibetans are just as apt to fall into the opposite extreme and may imagine robbers appearing and disappearing in deserts where no bandits ever put in an appearance.

A few days after my above-mentioned adventure with the robbers I happened to be in a valley when I was taken unawares by one of the many earthquakes which seem to become more and more frequent in Tibet at present. There was a terrific rumble and huge stones came thundering down on all sides.

I had to dodge quite a few stones to save my

life, and when the seismic disturbance reached its climax a few minutes later the earth reeled like a small boat in a gale and it was impossible to stand upright and dodge the stones without jumping about animal-fashion on hands and feet.

Some Tibetans a few hundred yards away were struck by big stones and apparently killed. When the earthquake was over I was surprised to see a Tibetan sit near the lifeless bodies of his colleagues without attempting even to find out whether they were actually dead.

When I approached him I saw that he was not hurt at all. He looked rather contented and complacent, like a man watching a beautiful sunrise. There was not the slightest sign of emotion about this man whose comrades had just been killed before his eyes.

I touched the bodies on the ground. The men were dead

"Your comrades are dead," I observed.

"Dead," said the complacent fellow. "Wait a little. They will stand up presently."

"But no," I said; "they are really dead. Their chests are crushed. They will never rise again."

"Wait until the ghost leaves me," said the Tibetan.

"What ghost?" I asked.

"The ghost who produced this hallucination," he answered.

It was obvious that he believed the whole calamity to be a mere hallucination brought about by an evil spirit who had appeared to him just before the earthquake had started.

So not only robbers, but even an earthquake with its terrific noise is not necessarily real to Tibetan eyes.

Like most other calamities, the Tibetans attribute earthquakes, when they do accept their reality, to the wrath of their gods who are irritated by the evil thoughts of human beings and send earthquakes or epidemics to punish the world.

I cannot help thinking that the robbers of Tibet are far from being the worst people to defy the wrath of the gods.

The bandits in Tibet take away from their victims only the things they can actually use, and nothing else. While civilized people seldom voluntarily put a limit to their selfishness and wait until this limit is drawn by others, Tibetan robbers do seem to keep their selfishness voluntarily within certain bounds.

On one occasion I was robbed by bandits at least a hundred miles distant from the nearest place where I could obtain food. Under the circumstances the Tibetan robbers did not confiscate all my food, but only a portion of it, leaving me a little so that I should not starve on the way.

Finally, the egotism of the Tibetan robbers does not seem to be of the boundless variety. It is crude, but it is not boundless.

CHAPTER IV

TIBETAN CIVILIZATION

I OFTEN happened to overhear talks—sometimes even confidential talks—of lamas and ordinary Tibetans, but soon after reaching the inhabited area I had the rare pleasure of overhearing a long conversation between three wealthy Tibetans wearing expensive turquoise ear-rings and accompanied by a large number of servants armed with sticks.

It is not pleasant for a poorly clad Tibetan to meet such wealthy people accompanied by their servants, as he may not step aside quickly enough, or forget to thrust out his tongue, which is considered a mark of respect in Tibet, or he may fail to stand up when important people wearing expensive ear-rings are passing, thus giving the servants a chance to ingratiate themselves with their masters by giving him a good licking.

I did not move out of the way when they approached, but when the servants learned from a few educated Tibetans who had just tried to talk to me that I was a "deaf-and-dumb traveller",

I was not molested by them, and the three Tibetan notabilities happened to stop and to talk within hearing distance of me.

With a majestic gesture the servants were sent away to buy food.

Rich Tibetans shout instead of talking, and they fairly roar instead of laughing. The greater the volume of a man's voice, the richer and the more powerful he is supposed to be in Tibet.

The wealthy Tibetans thought that they were quite alone, the "deaf-and-dumb traveller" being the only person within hearing distance. They lowered their voices and began to make jokes about the lamas while they cast suspicious glances in all directions, since the priests in Tibet are a very powerful body, a fact which even rich Tibetans are very wise to bear in mind.

"Yes," said one of them, "and this thing happened at X." (He mentioned a place in North-Eastern Tibet where the brigands, quite unlike the nice robbers in Western Tibet, are notorious for their cruelty.) "A few months ago the brigands did not hesitate to attack a lama."

"A lama!" exclaimed the other. "How extraordinary that they should not show a little more respect for their competitors!"

"When the robbers approached threateningly," continued the other, "they noticed that the lama was trembling with fear. Then one of the robbers said to him: 'What, holy man, *you* tremble? If someone kills me, *I* go straight to hell; but *you*, you go straight to paradise if I kill you—why do you tremble then?' 'It's true I should go to paradise,' answered the trembling lama, 'but *life is so nice after all*!'"

The three Tibetans laughed heartily, and their false silver teeth were clearly visible.

When distinguished Tibetans open their mouths, one can see pointed silver capsules covering their teeth. These silver capsules are the Tibetan equivalent of our gold crowns. Only rich Tibetans can afford artificial teeth.

"And what happened to the lama?" asked the other one.

"He had made the robbers laugh so much," came the answer, "that they did not hurt him at all."

At that moment the servants returned and the three Tibetan notabilities instantly stopped their jokes about the lamas. They probably did not care a straw for lamas, religion, or paradise, but thought it best to keep their opinion of the priesthood to themselves, it being much better for them if *others* believed in lamas and religion.

Now that they felt that their conversation was overheard, they became conventional and their talk was soon quite meaningless.

It would be a great mistake to suppose that

in the wide open spaces of Tibet, with their scarce population, all ceremonies, all make-believe, and all prejudices are non-existent. On the contrary, the Tibetans seem to be very punctilious on questions of etiquette. The few hundred wise men of Tibet seem to be the only Tibetans who do not care for any kind of make-belief.

Hospitable Tibetans of the wealthier class offer food to their guests again and again as soon as their bowl is empty, but woe to the man who takes this kind offer at face value if the invitation to help himself is extended a third time. No matter how great the appearance of sincerity, a third offer is intended to be a purely theatrical affair, and the guest filling up his bowl for a third time would be put down as an uneducated person. Tibetan nomads and other very simple folk have no time for such things, however, and with them such ceremonies and pretence are unnecessary.

Only young Tibetans occasionally revolt against insincerity and this playing of "theatre" in their daily lives, but in most cases they are soon forced into submission to the rules.

The education of the younger generation in Tibet is mostly catered for in the monasteries, although there are a few schools outside them. There the young Tibetans have to listen to many meaningless speeches and gradually the thing so boastingly called "education" distorts their boyish common sense, cripples their enthusiasm, and turns them into selfish little imitative machines that do everything precisely in the same way as it is done by everybody.

Young people, especially boys, in Tibet always instinctively desired my company. I am reasonably certain that no Tibetan youngster would have denounced me to the lamas had he found out that I was a white intruder. Older Tibetans might have done it. It is very difficult and painful to the young to be gradually forced into the grooves of Tibetan civilization with its many insufficiencies, traditions, and inner contradictions.

The sheepish attitude of the Tibetan masses is illustrated by the fact that the Tibetans never wash from birth to death. Although there are many lakes in Tibet, the population has "washed" with butter and mustard for centuries past. Everybody is doing what everybody else is doing, and once a thing has become traditional people cease to think whether a well-established habit is foolish or not.

The ways of the Tibetans are frightfully filthy. They often drink water flowing out from dunghills. It may happen that liquids from dead bodies come into direct contact with food.

On one occasion I was very kindly offered food prepared with knives which had been used a few hours before for cutting up a dead body. I refused to take it. The people present were greatly astonished that I was not hungry and none of them seemed to guess the reason why I had refused!

Often dung is picked up with the hands for use as fuel, and then the hands are not cleaned and food is put into the mouth with fingers sticky with dung. In some of the villages refuse is simply thrown out into the streets until it reaches up to the level of the roofs, thus literally burying the inhabitants in their own dirt.

Tibet thus ranks amongst the filthiest countries in the world, but the white traveller would do wrong to hold contempt for the Tibetans on account of their filthy habits and to feel superior to them on that account. It is true that the Tibetans are rather filthy *outwardly*, but they are probably cleaner where white people are often not clean at all, viz. in *their hearts*. White people are often scrupulously clean outwardly, but they may inwardly entertain many evil thoughts. I am sometimes able to feel people's thoughts to a small degree. That is why I did not suffer very much from the physical uncleanliness of Tibet. I do not mean to claim that the Tibetans are faultless. Far from it. But they are much more careful than white people not to harm themselves and their surroundings by evil thoughts. The spiritual aspect of things is much more seriously taken into account in Tibet than their material side. Thoughts and feelings are considered as realities, just as real as visible things and human actions. Such a conception does not usually occur to white people.

Even if they were given education in a Western sense on Western lines, I doubt whether the Tibetans would ever equal the white man intellectually. But they probably have finer intuition than most white people. Married people in Tibet, I imagine, have very little difficulty in finding out about how their husbands or wives are disposed to them.

It is difficult for a white person to penetrate into the marital secrets of the Tibetans. Viewing these matters superficially, I must say that I never saw a single instance of jealousy or a single matrimonial scene throughout my travel in Tibet, not even where several husbands were married to one wife, which is a fairly widely spread practice with Tibetan farmers, although uncommon amongst nomads.

In most parts of Tibet I ingratiated myself with young ladies by asking them in Tibetan:

"*Kyula tug-gu taka ʐando?*" i.e. How many children have you got?

This is a question you may put to any young lady in Tibet with perfect safety.

It is difficult to judge by outward signs the degree of affection people hold for the other members of their family. In one case, where someone had just died, the attitude of the nearest relatives seemed to me to be a little callous, judging by Western standards; but perhaps the Tibetans make an effort to hide their feelings in such circumstances. I saw tears of joy and emotion in Tibet, but hardly ever tears of sorrow.

Attending a Tibetan funeral is a terrible experience. I once had to do so. The Tibetan had been dead for several days. I learnt that the family were satisfied that his soul would rest in peace because he had had the good luck to die in the presence of a lama who had been called in time. The lama had sung certain queer songs which nobody could understand and then he had touched several times the crown of the dying man's head.

When a person is dying the lamas touch the crown of his head. It is a general belief in Tibet that this facilitates the escape of the soul from the body, the soul rising out of the body through the crown of the head.

Ever since the Tibetan had died the lama had remained seated near the dead body. Food was brought for both, that is to say for the dead man as well as for the lama. The latter ate really and the former symbolically. Funeral preparations are elaborate in Tibet. They constitute a considerable source of income for the Tibetan priesthood, who like to complicate matters as much as possible.

Finally the hour fixed for the funeral arrived. The lama performed elaborate rites and incantations. Then the dead body, without being put into a coffin or case, was carried out, the lama walking immediately behind it, while a small group of relatives and close friends followed at a certain distance.

We arrived at a place where many human bones were scattered in all directions. Large white or whitish stone slabs covered the ground.

The dead body was put on the ground and then two men armed with big knives began to cut up the body after stripping off the dead man's clothes and handing them respectfully to the lama, who took them as a funeral fee or a contribution towards his funeral fee.

During this ghastly scene no one cried, and no one amongst the relatives or friends present showed any visible sign of sorrow.

The pieces of flesh cut from the dead body were thrown out in a circle where a good many birds had gathered for this strange meal. Suddenly a few ravens mingled with the more respectable birds and began devouring the dead man's flesh. Since, however, ravens are disliked by the Tibetans, who do not seem to like the flesh from the bodies of their dead to go into such degraded bodies, a few of the people in the funeral party picked up stones and cast them at the ravens with great dexterity.

How did such ghastly funeral rites come into existence? There is an apparent reason for them. This method of disposing of the dead necessitates less work than burial, and cremation is impossible in most parts of Tibet owing to lack of wood. They could not burn their dead on a fire made of yak-dung, which commonly serves them as fuel. But there is also a deeper and much more valid reason for cutting up the Tibetan dead. Some of the wise men of Tibet gave me hints regarding the matter.

If dead bodies were not cut up soon after death, the Tibetans would be afraid that evil spirits might enter into them. Only in the case of very holy lamas of high rank do the Tibetans occasionally bury the dead bodies, after soaking them in molten butter. In the case of such holy people the evil spirits are supposed to be powerless. Moreover, such lamas are buried inside the monasteries where evil spirits are driven away again and again by an elaborate system of incantations. But in the case of ordinary

Tibetans, who are not so well protected, simple burial would be too dangerous.

Sometimes magicians who rule over hosts of evil spirits are credited with the power to send out an evil spirit with the mission of entering the body of a dead man. Only by radical destruction of human corpses can this purpose be foiled.

This belief is not specifically Tibetan. There are other countries in the world where the relatives of persons just buried even guard the tombs of their deceased with loaded guns—in Haiti, for instance—to prevent people versed in magic from getting hold of and misusing the corpses before the latter have reached an advance stage of putrefaction.

Very often human bones are used in Tibet. Prayer mills, censers, and sometimes whole aprons are made of human bones. At times, too, magicians use sticks to which one or a whole range of human skulls are attached.

Now, after reading all this the reader should not imagine that the Tibetans think they live in an uncivilized country. Like most other people, they have a very high opinion of themselves, and their opinion about themselves seems only to be higher the less they happen to know about others.

There are even Tibetans who consider Tibet the most civilized country in the world, which reminds one of the saying of the French writer who defined civilization as *"ce qui est près de nous"*.

Some Tibetans are even of the opinion that poor barren Tibet is the most fertile country and the garden of the world, and that is why her bad neighbours cast covetous eyes on Tibet. In the eyes of many Tibetans Tibet is just as powerful a country as England or Russia. I was surprised to hear a lama refer to the Younghusband Expedition as the "Great War between Tibet and India"!

The broad masses of the Tibetans, however, do not seem to care much for the position of Tibet in the world. They consider all questions of power as part of the material aspect of things, and matter for them is something negligible. Hence their utter indifference to improvements of their material condition and to the very idea of progress in a Western sense.

Like two-thirds of the population of India, nearly all Tibetans believe in reincarnation. They believe that in the past they lived on this earth in other bodies and that they will come back to this earth in other bodies again and again. They consider their lives to be a mere day in a much longer existence extending over millions of years, the soul, after a period of rest, passing again into the body of a new-born child.

It is believed that a grown-up person spends many hundred years in paradise or hell according to the virtues amassed or sins committed in the last existence before having squared his accounts relative to the past existence by pleasure or pain. Then his soul descends into the body of a newborn child again. Children, however, on meeting an untimely death, have no accounts to settle in heaven or hell and are reborn therefore almost immediately. Such souls, according to the Tibetans, often carry the memory of the last incarnation over into the new existence, and if one believes the Tibetans it often happens that quite a young child distinctly remembers having been a child in a neighbouring village, and when it is taken to the place described as the place of his previous existence he will recognize his father and mother, his toys, household utensils, clothes, and the like; and his former parents and relatives will confirm the veracity of his statements. Cases of this kind are far too frequent in Tibet to be accounted for by the convenient explanation of a plot preconcerted by the many people concerned in order to become the topic of gossip in the district.

The holier a person, the Tibetans say, the more he or she is likely to remember details from his or her previous incarnations. Even if the memory of past incarnations is lost in later life, the Tibetans say that it exists to a certain degree at the age of seven in the case of souls of a higher degree of evolution.

Going by this rule and claiming that they are holy, practically all the lamas declare that they can remember their past incarnations. On the other hand, I never heard any of the wise men of Tibet, who for the most part live outside the monasteries, say anything about their past incarnations. They may remember them, but are very reluctant to talk about them. These men *are* holy. It is not necessary for them, therefore, to make an effort to *appear holy* and to emphasize their holiness by stories of past incarnations and pretended memories of past incarnations.

What is the actual basis for this belief in reincarnation which is so common in the East? Is there logical justification for it?

This is how one of the wise hermits of Tibet explained it to me in his clear and lucid manner:

"Can life spring from something that is not life?" he asked.

"No," I replied.

"If the soul of man is created out of nothing," he went on, "it is likely to go back into nothing."

"If we shall live for ever in the future," observed another wise hermit, "we must have lived always in the past."

Reincarnation is a lofty symbol of the oneness of life. If the idea of reincarnation is approached with an open heart and mind, the illusion of separating the "I" from the "non-I" disappears. The "I" and the "non-I" are really the same thing, and it is just as foolish to treat that which is not "I" in a way different to the way one treats one's "I", as it would be foolish to treat one's left arm in a way different to one's right arm.

But the illusion of the I-consciousness is very tenacious. The "I" eagerly snatches anything, be it even a floating piece of straw, to nourish its self-centredness. A bigoted conception of reincarnation tends to strengthen the false I-consciousness and it subtly increases the division between the "I" and the "non-I". When the idea of reincarnation is not approached with an open heart and mind, and when it is used to give comfort to the "I" by holding out a promise of its continuation after death, the division between the "I" and the "non-I" is subtly strengthened. Only when every notion of gaining or getting is discarded and reincarnation stands out *as a lofty symbol* and *not as a safety-belt for the "I"*, can it help to break down the false egocentrical conception of life.

Reincarnation should be a lofty symbol. In actual fact, in most cases it is merely used as a safety-belt for the "I". If an individual abstains from doing harm to others because he thinks he will get a good incarnation in future by doing so, he transplants the materialistic attitude of gaining and getting into the spiritual sphere. This is no longer spirituality but materialistic spirituality or spiritual materialism, i.e. the very reverse of real spirituality.

A bigoted and egocentrical conception of reincarnation, by the way, is fundamentally similar to any other bigoted conception of religion. What is the difference between a person who is afraid to commit an evil action from fear of hell and a person abstaining from committing an evil action from fear of a bad reincarnation? Many people who have adopted an orthodox theosophical conception of life think they are more advanced or more religious than people having an orthodox belief in some of the dogmatic religions. But they are mistaken. They have only changed the form but not the contents. Fundamentally they still hold the same beliefs in another form.

The lofty Hindu teachings of old speak of the Divine, the ever-present, immovable Spirit of the Universe that passes all understanding, that can only be understood as a principle of eternal oneness as opposed to the turmoil of manifestation.

The spirit of these teachings has been corrupted. The idea of reincarnation expressed the oneness of life as a lofty symbol.

It is accepted in a narrow-minded and bigoted spirit, and in practice the reincarnation idea is turned into a safety-belt for the "I".

In all probability it is this bigoted conception of the idea of reincarnation which makes the population of Tibet and the non-Mohammedan section of the population of India so indolent and careless in the sphere of material activity. They have time and lots of time for everything. "Things will work themselves out in the next incarnation," they say. Anyhow, all eternity is before them in which to solve their problems. In all probability that is why they do not live so much in the present.

CHAPTER V

THE STRANGE DOINGS OF THE LAMAS

GREAT caution was necessary whenever I visited a Tibetan monastery. To have been found out by the lamas would have been a terrible experience. I do not think they would have killed me, since human life is nearly always respected in Tibet. But I doubt whether I should have been able to find my way out of any monastery had I been taken prisoner by the lamas.

As I practically never walked about alone in the monasteries, but joined groups of other pilgrims, I knew in most cases what to do at a given moment so as not to attract attention, and since I carefully maintained the pose of a deaf-and-dumb person whilst inside a monastery, the lamas could not detect me on account of my foreign accent.

These rambles through Tibetan monasteries were most interesting in spite of the fact that some of the secret rooms and sanctuaries are not accessible to pilgrims.

The monasteries usually contain ornaments of considerable value and costly libraries. The most sacred books are kept under canopies, reminding one somewhat of the canopies carried about in Catholic processions. Other rooms contain gigantic reproductions of objects considered most indecent in Western countries, some of them measuring six feet in height.

On one occasion I had a very narrow escape from being found out by the lamas.

I had waited for other pilgrims in order to join them for a visit to some of the sanctuaries. But there happened to be none who were just about to visit the place I particularly wished to visit, and since my time was limited—I intended to spend only eight hours in the monastery—I finally decided to walk about alone, a thing I had formerly done on rare occasions only.

I entered a very large room where three statues representing many-handed and many-legged Divinities stood in a row at one end of the room. As I thought I was quite alone I walked about, much as does a tourist visiting a museum in a Western country. I approached the statues and carefully examined their eyes. I had a vague suspicion that the lamas often hide somebody inside the statues of their Divinities and I hoped to find a secret entrance somewhere by which the lamas entered them. Not having found any such entrance on the front side, I walked round the row of statues to have a good look at them from behind.

I had not gone many yards before ten or fifteen secret doors were thrown open in the walls of the room and about two dozen lamas rushed out and instantly surrounded me. The lamas had watched me from behind the wall. To make things worse, I had circumambulated the statues in the wrong direction. The Tibetans always walk round their idols from left to right, showing them reverently the right side of their bodies. I had done precisely the contrary. I had walked round them from right to left, which no real Tibetan would ever dream of doing!

The crowd of lamas became still more suspicious when they found that I was deaf and dumb, and did not answer any of the many questions showered on me like a hail-storm.

To make things still worse, one of the lamas proposed to look into my eyes in order to "cure me". My blue eyes had always been a danger throughout my travels in Tibet. I could have dyed my eyes too, but, as I have stated elsewhere, I did not want to run the risk of doing harm to them by continual dyeing. And now the very fact that I was most anxious to hide was to become the object of close scrutiny by this large crowd of suspicious priests.

Only happy presence of mind saved me. I knew that according to Tibetan ideas of religion it is a dreadful crime to disturb a holy man while he prays. Then and there I sat down and went into a state of deep and motionless meditation with closed eyes.

The lamas were powerless. None of them dared to approach me. But they remained standing about, waiting patiently for my prayer to come to an end.

It was difficult to guess what opinion they had formed of me. They had probably never seen a white person in their lives, but nevertheless my behaviour had been much too strange not to put them on their guard.

So it became a matter of patience. I hoped that if I went on meditating for several hours the lamas finally would become convinced that I was really a holy pilgrim. But as the hours rolled by the situation became more desperate. After a couple of hours the crowd had increased considerably and more and more lamas had come to have a good look at the "holy man". Finally respectful shouts were heard of *"mkhan-po"*, *"mkhan-po"*. It was the abbot in person who came along to see the "saint". He looked very impressive in his tapering head-gear, which I could clearly see through my half-closed eyes, and after glancing at me he passed on majestically.

It is indescribably painful for a white man to sit in exactly the same position for many hours at a stretch, since Westerners are not used to the particular type of religious exercise. But time does not matter in the Orient—certain religious or pseudo-religious practices in the East start by seven years' silence, so that matter is a negligible one in Tibetan monasteries—and after several hours the crowd still stood there and gaped almost open-mouthed.

To make the situation all the more critical, one of the plugs in my nostrils, which I had stuck in for the purpose of widening them and to give my nose a more genuine Tibetan aspect, began to get loose and, as the slightest movement would have been interpreted by the lamas as meaning the cessation of my pious contemplations, I could not push it back with my hand. Had the plug actually come out, a merely fifty per cent Tibetan nose would have meant the finishing-stroke. Fortunately the plug did not fall out after all.

After about five hours of staring the time at last came when the lamas were due to take their meal. They were hungry and their appetites proved stronger than their suspicion and curiosity. I had hoped that they would all go away and leave me alone, so that I could make my escape.

At the last moment, however, I was disappointed in this. After some discussion, two of the most suspicious lamas insisted on one of them remaining behind to keep an eye on me while the others went away to eat.

Now my situation had become quite desperate. Flight was impossible. The nearest of the four gates of the monastery was several hundred yards distant. Had I jumped up and run away the lama watching me would not have failed to raise the alarm and the gates would have been closed long before I could have reached them.

On the other hand, I could not continue my profound devotions much longer. The pain in all my limbs was dreadful. Sooner or later I must finish. But what then? As soon as I made the slightest movement the examination by the lamas would begin again and it would not take long before I should be in custody.

Then an almost miraculous thing happened.

A side-door opened quietly and a solitary lama stepped out. In appearance he looked like other lamas, but one felt vaguely that he must be quite a different being. Slowly he walked up to the "guard". He began to talk to him and led him away. Before they had both disappeared, the lama who had obviously come out to help me gave me a stealthy sign with his left hand: "Go."

I was saved! Five minutes later I was beyond the walls of the monastery.

The lama who had come out from the side-door must have been one of the wise men of Tibet living in the monastery as a lama. Maybe he was wise enough to know that I meant no harm in Tibet.

This was the second time that I was saved during my journey by some quite unexpected intervention.

The first experience of a similar kind I had had in Turkistan, not far from Chotan. Suddenly a horseman, looking majestic and yet humble, had appeared to warn me of a small detachment of cavalry which was out to capture me. I had hidden immediately at the place indicated by the mysterious horseman. The cavalry looked for me in vain—and the mysterious horseman turned out to be unknown to everybody in the district.

There are not many Tibetans who would dare to disturb a holy man while he is in a state of pious meditation. Terrible punishment after death would be meted out to a person committing so heinous an offence. The Tibetans think that an abrupt cessation of deep meditation may too suddenly call down the meditating person from the celestial spheres into full consciousness of his materialistic surroundings, and this violent waking-up of a person plunged into a state of what we in the West may call deep trance may be most harmful to him.

Punishment for disturbing a meditating person is—hell. The Tibetan hells are much more uncomfortable than our Western hell—I mean the hell where people are afraid they will go after death. (Many people have already made a hell of this life in the West.) Tibet is a cold country and even in summer it is really warm only in the afternoons. The Tibetans therefore suffer much from exposure to cold, and they might consider a hot hell after death a pleasant change. The practical lamas, who have every interest that people should be as much afraid of hell as possible, have introduced therefore the idea of a cold hell, so that everybody may be afraid according to his particular taste.

About a week after the experience within the monastery I attended a rather ghastly show in another monastery. It was very carefully staged, and I heard that the lamas had rehearsed the show day after day for a whole year. So everything went off very smoothly. The lamas danced in the central court of the monastery. They wore grotesque masks representing evil spirits which looked so awful and so live that the Tibetan crowd literally trembled with terror. The lamas wore bright clothes and an exact copy of the dreadful masks they had on their faces appeared painted on their chests. From the opposite side of the yard there came a procession of sinners, looking thin, miserable, and terror-stricken. The procession broke up, making rhythmical movements of terror. Each sinner was attacked by a host of demons which chased him, while the poor victim shrieked terribly and ran faster and faster. Finally he stood still and writhed in agony while several dozen demons seized him.

A queer music, more rhythmical than tuneful, accompanied the scenes. The whole thing was most realistic and made a deep impression not only on the Tibetans but, I must confess, also on the author who watched the proceedings from a corner. I am sure that if the lamas cared to come to the West they could greatly impress a Western audience with this show. The scenes were so striking and well acted that even the enlightened public of the West would not remain indifferent.

By such shows the lamas keep alive the fear of hell.

Uncomfortable as it is, the Tibetan hell, however, is *not eternal*. The lamas do not state precisely how long it lasts, since, as they put it, "time only pertains to the material world. The world of spirit is timeless". Heaven and hell come in between two successive incarnations, and as soon as the soul of the departed has stayed long enough in heaven or hell to get the reward for his good deeds or the punishment for his sins, it returns to earth to be reborn into the body of a child and start a new existence.

Some of the lamas show understanding for these deeper things. According to the lamas whom I heard preach on these matters, a human being is threefold and consists of three parts, viz.: (*a*) his gross body; (*b*) a subtle invisible body connected with the gross body and continually modified and influenced through the senses; and (*c*) the individual soul, which is a part of the spirit pervading the whole universe and unchanging and incorruptible by its very nature.

When a person dies the subtle invisible body together with the individual soul leaves the gross body. The less materially-minded the dying person is, the easier becomes this process of discarding the gross body. But the lamas point out that nearly all persons are at least to a degree materially-minded, and it is advisable, therefore, that a lama should be called when somebody is about to die, since by pious songs and prayers, the reciting of some magic words, and knocking at the crown of the head of the dying person he may facilitate the painful process of evacuation of the physical body.

During life, thoughts and feelings continually influence the subtle invisible body, and after death it retains a taint of all these impressions.

It is this subtle body, allied to the soul, that goes to heaven or hell according to the sins or merits of the departed. There, a slow process of disintegration takes place. Every kind or unkind thought, word, or action during life has left some impression on the invisible body, and these impressions must be removed after death by suffering or by enjoyment. As this process of squaring accounts continues, the invisible body disintegrates more and more, until nothing but the unchanging and incorruptible soul, which is a part of the world-soul, remains and again returns to earth to enter the body of a new-born child.

I was curious to find out what the lamas thought of the actual aspect and constitution of the subtle invisible body. As I only conversed with the common people and the Tibetan hermits (about whom I shall write in the last two chapters of this book), and never addressed the lamas, since the latter are much more dangerous than all their cold and hot hells put together, I had to listen to numerous talks to pupils and occasional conversations between the lamas themselves to find out something more about the matter.

However, it seems to me that when the lamas no longer talk vaguely about the subtle invisible body, but begin to provide details, their concrete descriptions of its actual aspect and characteristics vary a great deal. One lama whom I heard speaking declared that the subtle body consisted of invisible ethers which circulated at great speed, so fast in fact that the sight of them "made a clairvoyant's head turn". The invisible ethers circulate in a very large number of small vessels which run out from a common centre.

When a pupil asked how many such vessels existed, the lama answered: 72,000. But I distinctly remember another lama having said in reply to precisely the same question that the number of vessels in the subtle body was 7272 *bum* (1 *bum* = 100,000), that is to say 727,200,000.

In answer to the questions of pupils as to where the centre of the vessels is located, the answers given by various lamas in different monasteries were far from being identical. One lama said it was in the heart, another said it was in the navel, and a third said that the centre shifted according to the varying corporeal characteristics of the individual in question!

Seeing that all these contradictions exist, it is small wonder that most lamas adopt an abstruse and ambiguous way of expressing their thoughts, and complicate matters whenever their pupils begin to put concrete questions. The wise men of Tibet are different. Their answers are always simple and straightforward. *They never try to complicate matters.* In most cases the latter course is only resorted to by people who are anxious to cover up their ignorance or who wish to mislead or take advantage of others.

The reader need not imagine that most lamas are interested in these deeper things. Those who approach such matters at all are only a small minority. Most lamas are very ignorant. All they can tell the people is to recommend them to murmur as often as possible the four holy words, "*Om Mani Padme Hum*", as every time these six holy syllables are murmured "a thousand sins are forgiven you". Apart from murmuring the holy formula, confession of sins is a widespread practice in Tibetan monasteries and, seeing the practical and businesslike ways of the lamas, I do not doubt that confession by telephone will be unhesitatingly authorized by them as soon as Tibet adopts telephonic communication on a large scale. Perhaps there will then be an extra charge for confessing sins to the *mkhan-po* (the abbot) direct, this method of confession being considered a little more efficacious by the Tibetans.

Often the abbots of Tibetan monasteries are former business men or local governors, and in some cases even former brigands! Having become abbots, they make an effort to be good and virtuous because they think it pays spiritually to be good and virtuous. They thus transplant their materialistic attitude of grabbing and getting into the spiritual sphere—a common illusion of many people who call themselves spiritual.

The abbots have extensive powers. They see to it that the monks behave properly and that they have no association with women. It is the abbot who distributes the property of the monastery, which is sometimes considerable, as the population of each neighbouring district is forced to pay nearly half of their income as a tax to the monastery, the leaders of which in most cases do not seem to care a straw for the other Tibetan authorities and which are often a veritable state within the state. It is the abbot who looks after the distribution of food in the large depot which exists in most monasteries and is supplied chiefly with dried meat. Dried meat keeps good for years in Tibet without necessitating any special method of preservation.

The main article of food in most monasteries is dried meat and yet it is formally forbidden to Buddhists to eat meat!

This seems to be a contradiction, but in Tibet the lamas are *always right*. They have a collection of holy books containing 108 volumes, each volume weighing something like ten pounds. So it is not difficult for them to find suitable texts to excuse everything they do by taking the *letter* of their complicated religious texts and overlooking their *spirit*.

DOINGS OF THE LAMAS

The lamas do not deny that it is written again and again in Buddhist holy scripture: "Thou shalt not kill. Thou shalt not eat any meat." But, nevertheless, they eat meat. They simply say that "if a man wants to kill animals for food he should ask a priest to be present when the animal is killed. Thus the sin of killing will be forgiven to him."

I may add in this connection that practically all the wise hermits of Tibet, who in their humble abode have not a single religious text, but who live the spirit of the living Buddha, are vegetarians. This is only possible, of course, for Tibetans who manage to live on very, very small quantities of food.

In most cases no women—apart from old nuns with shaven heads—are allowed to enter a monastery, and even when they leave the monastery for a short time, normal sex indulgence is made very difficult for the lamas. There are exceptions, especially in the case of the red-cap lamas who are even allowed to marry, but the most powerful sect, which has by far the largest number of adherents, the yellow-cap sect, is very strict in enforcing chastity of the lamas by making all contact with women impossible.

Many things a Westerner would call unnatural go on, therefore, within the walls of a Tibetan monastery. Those who have travelled in the

Orient may know that the Oriental view is much more lenient than the Western one. The number of lamas having formed a certain type of union with one of the younger lamas seems to be considerable, and in some monasteries conditions in this respect are such that even a solitary pilgrim is not immune from certain unmistakable invitations extended by some young lamas. Although it would be too much to say that these practices are general, it is obvious that they are fairly frequent.

On one occasion when I walked about in the company of a few other pilgrims we saw a happening which would make an average Westerner repeat "Shocking!" for several weeks in succession. The Tibetans were hardly upset at all. While they calmly discussed the matter I of course reserved my opinion, as I never opened my mouth within the precincts of a monastery.

"This is somewhat unusual," observed one of the Tibetans calmly.

"I never thought the lamas could do such a thing," returned another.

"Do not forget," put in a third pilgrim, "that the lamas are very wise. Even if they do a thing that seems strange to us, they do it for the good of the world."

"I have always been told not to find fault with a lama's actions," said the first pilgrim.

"Perhaps these two lamas are very holy," returned the third pilgrim. "They were coming too near to Nirvana and as they wanted to remain in their bodies so as to be able to help the world, they voluntarily committed a sin in a spirit of sacrifice."

A devout silence would follow the conversation. The Tibetan pilgrims would look very sheepish and credulous and I had to take some pains to conceal my merriment.

It seems improbable that the lamas conceal women inside the monasteries. Especially, the existence of white women, living with hundreds of rather filthy-looking lamas with whom they are infatuated, seems to me exceedingly improbable. I sometimes wonder what a lama would look like when meeting suddenly a nice young European or American girl in a monastery. He would probably mistake her for a ghost.

Most Tibetans are terribly afraid of evil spirits and they people their whole surroundings with them. When ghosts do much mischief, the lamas are supposed to be the only ones who can offer assistance by driving them away with magic incantations and prayers. There are innumerable millions of evil spirits, but they can be classed, there being 360 different varieties. Cataloguing all these evil spirits and learning all their names and evil characteristics and the best method of fighting them is a matter of absorbing study to many Tibetan priests. They have built up the knowledge of ghosts into an imposing scientific structure which greatly baffles the ignorant masses.

As about twenty per cent of the population of Tibet are priests and monks, it is rather difficult for all these people to make a living. Where the taxes levied by the priests, the fees for praying and exorcizing, the income from funeral rites, the sale of talismans, and the gifts of numerous pilgrims are not sufficient to keep the lamas going, they invent a local Divinity having a particularly wrathful and difficult temper which must be propitiated continually to keep away evil influences from the district in question. The people living there naturally defray the expense of those propitiatory practices considered absolutely necessary by the priests "in the interests of the people".

The lamas even exploit children. When they are about eight to ten years old the future priests are sent to the monasteries. According to Tibetan ideas a boy is old enough to become the pupil of a priest when he is big enough to scare away a bird of moderate size. The children coming from well-to-do families are treated nicely, but those from poor families are often maltreated and sent out by their teachers to beg, the money collected by them being afterwards taken away by their teachers. One cannot imagine the Buddha treating a poor boy in a way different from a rich one, but "his" priests often do so. Their prayers are often selfish. Buddha himself could not possibly have encouraged prayers for egotistical purposes, as they turn religion into a farce.

When agricultural districts in Tibet are threatened by the effects of drought, the farmers pay something to a few hundred priests who organize processions praying for rain, but people building houses in the same districts want the fine weather to continue, and they pay something to other priests so that they should go about praying for dry weather. Thus hundreds of priests pray simultaneously for rain and for dry weather, which must put their gods into a very embarrassing position, as in spite of all their power they cannot give rain and sunshine at the same time.

We may laugh at this, but many civilized people in the West are doing precisely the same thing. Real religion is *love*. It has nothing to do with such comedies. He who lives the *spirit* of his religion and not only five minutes a week after listening to some uplifting sermon, but every moment of his life, has no God whom he tries to coax and to bribe; he has not "his" God whom he tries to use as a weapon against his neighbour.

Many Tibetan lamas have their own Divinity whose name they keep secret—their *own* god, mind you—with whom they want to keep the monopoly of entering into contact!

It is just the latter type of Tibetan priest who is not always kind in the little things of his daily life. The same applies to many pilgrims, who advance by throwing themselves flat on the ground every two yards and sometimes cover distances of one or two hundred English miles by throwing themselves on the ground every two yards. But woe to the pilgrim who is taken ill during such a pilgrimage! His pious colleagues may leave him behind without any help. There is no text *formally* ordering a pilgrim to help another pilgrim taken ill on the way. And every time he throws himself to the ground a Tibetan pilgrim, if I may say so, expects some sort of credit entry into his book of virtues. He is very anxious, therefore, not to interrupt his meritorious crawling exercises no matter what happens.

The Tibetan robbers never throw themselves to the ground to acquire merit. They do not make any effort to be good and, unlike the pilgrims, they do not even imagine that they are good. Yet, if a member of a gang of Tibetan robbers is taken ill on the way, he is *not* left behind without any help, but receives assistance.

The Tibetan pilgrims, on the whole, seem to be rather sheepish people. They mostly travel in flocks, as they are afraid of brigands and evil spirits.

Once, a group of at least twenty-five pilgrims ran away when they saw me approaching them in the lone solitudes of mysterious Tibet. They were greatly terrified on seeing a lonely man whom they evidently mistook for a ghost. The faster I approached, the faster the twenty-five adults ran away. I positively felt like a giant routing a whole army.

Only a pilgrim can enter practically all the monasteries of Tibet. Even a permit issued by the Government of the country would not enable an explorer to enter all the monasteries, especially those situated a long way from the capital. But the pilgrim is always welcome, as the lamas would never turn away a prospective customer.

During the course of centuries the lamas have created a curious blend of business and religion. The day Tibet introduces an industry on Western lines the lamas will probably not hesitate to set up whole batteries of prayer-mills driven by electricity and start a prayer subscription business on a large scale. They are so practical that where religious texts are very long they make several dozens of lamas read out several dozen pages at the same time, each lama reading a *different* page.

Thus, apart from very few exceptions, only the letter of Buddhism prevails and not its spirit.

The spirit of the living Buddha is nowadays to be found mostly *outside* the monasteries with some of the Tibetan hermits about whom I shall write in the last two chapters of this book, but here and there a few priests still remain in the monasteries who live up to the spirit of the living Buddha. In most cases these sincere men are treated as heretics by their more businesslike colleagues.

For sincere and uncompromising lamas may remind the other lamas how far they have departed from the spirit of the teachings of the Buddha. "Rites and ceremonies are unnecessary," taught the Buddha. "Using occult powers for healing or exorcizing is a great religious error." That passage is to be found in old authentic Buddhist writings. No wonder that most lamas dislike the presence of men who may remind them of such facts.

Specially consecrated food is kept in many temples. The lamas occasionally distribute pills made of rice, butter, and flour, and they claim that such magical rites ensure close contact with the Divinities. Although the historical Buddha never said he was divine and only spoke of the divine in *man*, the divine which is potentially in the heart of *every* human being, dogmatic Buddhism has turned not only Buddha himself into a god but also his relatives. Lamaistic Buddhism has developed the worship of the

Mother of Buddha. In many monasteries there are statues of the lamaistic Mother of God holding the infant Buddha in her arms. This worship of the Mother of Buddha was gradually elaborated by the Buddhist priesthood throughout the ages. No traces of it can be found in the early centuries of Buddhism.

There was no religious hierarchy at all during the first few centuries following the death of the Buddha. There were only some poor group leaders trying to keep alive the spirit of his teaching in the face of ever-increasing religious quackery destined to kill his *spirit* and to *distort his words* for the purpose of building up a system for selfish purposes and spiritual exploitation.

And there was no successor of Buddha during the first centuries following his death. Nor was there any hierarchical order amongst the group leaders.

It was only after the victory of Mahā-yana that the self-styled successors and "vice-gods" appeared. Mahā-yana was based on the assumption that the "real message of Buddha was too pure and elevated to have a chance of being rapidly accepted by the masses", and that therefore some sort of "watered-down Buddhism" should be created for the broad masses, thus ensuring the rapid victory of Buddhism as a system.

This was done. And Buddhism spread all

right, but it was no longer the Buddhism of Buddha.

If Buddha really intended to create a dogmatic religion and an organized belief, why on earth did he not write down his rules himself? Surely a man of the genius of Buddha and brought up as a son of a king knew how to write!

But the greatest initiators of the past have never written a line. They probably realized the fact that living realities cannot be imprisoned in texts.

Organized Buddhism, as it stands today, is a formidable machinery for exercising power by exploiting fear and credulity, especially "Buddhism" as it is in Tibet and Nepal.

Religion has been perverted more and more in order to establish the authority of its representatives.

The lamas are supposed to know everything. When a Tibetan wants advice he goes to the lamas. Even in matters connected with love and matrimony the lamas are consulted, and in many cases the Tibetans then go to unmarried lamas of the yellow-cap sect who are strictly forbidden to associate with women.

The Tibetans, on the whole, like to be told what to do. This prevents unnecessary thinking. The lamas greatly profit by this attitude.

When a Tibetan puts a question to a lama and the latter does not know what to say, the lama often acts like a Western physician I know when he is unable to diagnose a disease. He makes an effort to look very wise without saying anything.

When asked for advice in a complicated and difficult case, the lamas behave like certain Western lawyers when they are asked to give an opinion on a particularly uncertain and complicated legal issue : they talk a lot without saying anything definite.

The lamas are rather tricky and always manage to wriggle out of tight corners somehow with undiminished authority.

Here is a verbatim report, freely translated into English, of three conversations I overheard in Tibet :

I

The questioner went to a lama who, like many other Tibetan priests, was reputed to be a clairvoyant. He wished to know what was happening to one of his relatives living far away.

Questioner : "Is he going on well now ?"
Lama : "His condition is no longer exactly the same as it was some time ago."
Questioner : "Shall I see him again ?"
Lama : "That rests with the gods."

II

Conversation between a lama and a Tibetan who would like to know something about his brother living at a village at a distance of a few hundred miles.

Lama: "And I am quite certain that you have received news from him immediately, have you not?"

Customer: "No, Holy Father, I have not."

Lama (with unruffled composure): "Well, then you will hear from him soon!"

Customer: "I am ever so much obliged to you."

III

A critically minded Tibetan comes to a lama to protest.

Customer: "Last month many of you, reverend lamas, offered prayers for rain. Then it rained."

Lama: "But of course it rained. We prayed for rain and the gods deigned to answer our prayers."

Customer: "But this time we again brought you much butter, asking you to pray for rain. And this time there was no rain at all."

Lama: "You cannot question the will of the gods. The gods always know best."
Customer: "But what shall we do?"
Lama: "Bring us more butter and we shall pray again."

Meditation is widely practised in Tibet. It is easy to describe a meditating lama, but it is much more difficult to guess what is going on behind his lifeless face.

The meditating lama is seated motionless with bent legs and crossed arms. He keeps his eyes closed. His face is extraordinarily pale and thin. It more often resembles a statue made of wax than a human face, it is so absolutely colourless and lifeless. In this pose the lama remains seated for many hours, and in some exceptional cases for many days at a stretch. The longer a lama manages to remain in such a state of meditation, the greater is his reputation for holiness. Shrewd and practical lamas may be suspected, therefore, of remaining in this saintly position much longer than is really necessary for bringing to a conclusion their pious contemplations.

What is going on inside the head of a lama while he meditates? What is the object of his contemplation?

Many lamas are very ignorant and I cannot help thinking that they do not think at all while they contemplate. Their state of meditation may mean to them merely a meritorious state of isolation and fasting, and their contemplations may not convey to them anything at all. However, not all the lamas are in that position. Some Buddhist priests have a very definite object in view when they meditate, namely the concentration and hoarding of spiritual energy.

I must confess that all my observations in Tibetan monasteries, where I always painstakingly maintained the pose of a deaf-and-dumb pilgrim, never provided a real key to the purpose and mechanism of those meditation exercises. It was only when I met the wise men of Tibet, about whom I am writing in Chapters VI and VII of this book, that I got valuable hints regarding the matter.

The wise hermits of Tibet consider these contemplation exercises practised by the lamas as a *false* method of acquiring spirituality. Spirituality in their opinion must be the result of man's inner attitude to life. It must be *spontaneous*, and not "acquired" by any special methods or practices. The wise men of Tibet never go into a special pose to meditate. They never kneel down, either, nor do they have a special pose for praying. The wise men of Tibet do not pray only on certain occasions. *Their whole life is a prayer*.

The lamas, on the other hand, have built up an

elaborate system of meditation and prayer which they complicate more and more. Here is a list of some of the holy states of meditation practised in the monasteries. Please note that this list of contemplations is not even complete. There are thousands of others.

Contemplation having genuinely majestic and victorious characteristics.
Progressive contemplation in pursuance to holy principles.
Contemplation generously filling all the heavens.
Indestructible meditation.
Never-perishing contemplation.
Contemplation of absolute immobility.
Inexhaustible meditation.
Lightning contemplation.
Joy-giving contemplation.
Meditation which passes all objects of sensorial perception.
Meditation which eliminates all doubts in a radical manner.
Meditation which is past the effect of all joys and sorrows.
Highly instructive meditation of the Lion.
Victorious meditation of the majestic Moon.
Contemplation creating radiant light.
Meditation which does not look for anything.
Contemplation without intellectual activity.
Contemplation of immaculate brilliancy.
Contemplation of immeasurable light.
All-illuminating contemplation.
Meditation of majestic wisdom.
Contemplation which leaves no possible choice.
Meditation which never grows dim.
Meditation transcending all forms of existence.
Contemplation which has found a perceptible expression,

Meditation of consciously desired immobility of the intellect.
Meditation of definite liberation and non-attachment.
Meditation which gives freedom from attachment to things mundane.
Contemplation leading to detachment from things terrestrial,

and so forth and so on. Doubtless enumeration of all these various forms of meditation, together with several hundred others not included in the above list, gives a Buddhist priest in Tibet the reputation of a very learned man. The lamas obviously like to complicate matters.

How different are the wise men of Tibet. They never complicate things.

"Real meditation," one of these holy men—who, by the way, never call themselves holy—told me, "real meditation is a natural and effortless thing, not a fight to oust all thoughts which are conflicting with the specific thoughts one wants to dwell on at a specific time in order to get something in return for one's meditation, either materially or spiritually."

He put it much simpler, but as these intimate spiritual contacts were more on spiritual planes than on intellectual ones, I present these dialogues in a way which is more readily understood by the Western reader.

The meditation of the lamas—apart from very

rare exceptions in the case of lamas of the hermit type who can meditate truly, but do not need meditation at all—is of two different kinds. It is either no meditation, a mere posing and sitting motionless to acquire the reputation of holiness by pious dozing and napping, or it is the meditation of the "fighting type" so aptly described later in this book by my Tibetan hermit friend.

The purpose of lamaistic meditation is to uplift man from the "lower" world of matter into the "higher" world of the spirit. It ultimately tends to separate spirit from matter, just as the ultra-materialistic attitude to life so common in the West tends to separate matter from spirit. Both attitudes, if I may say so with respect, are equally foolish.

In so-called "meditation" all ideas coming up during the course of meditation which are not in line with the "holy" thoughts desired by the meditating lama are *driven away* by mental pictures which are antagonistic to the mental image desired by the lama. The Tibetan hermits who had lived in monasteries at more or less remote periods of their lives were in a position to give me valuable information on the matter.

The meditating lama goes to a secluded spot (where such is available). If not, he merely isolates himself mentally, wherever he happens to be. He then assumes the holy position, taking great care that his spine should be quite erect in one line with his neck, and that the point of his nose should be just above his navel. Whenever he lacks concentration and feels that his thoughts begin to wander, he looks at his navel. Whenever he gets sleepy he begins to look at the upper part of his nose.

All thoughts which are not "holy" and happen to rise up during "meditation" must be ruthlessly fought by appropriate mental images.

The most usual thoughts disturbing the peace of meditating lamas are said to be thoughts of lust. This seems natural. The sex-life of the lamas is crippled in most cases, and desires which people do not dare to satisfy out of fear rather than out of deeper understanding have a tendency to leave the consciousness and to get a firm hold on the subconsciousness. When a lama starts meditation he first makes his mind a "blank". And whenever our mind is "blank", the subconsciousness sets to work at once and all those hidden unwanted thoughts creep to the surface.

When the meditating lama is thus assailed by sensual thoughts, he must *fight* those mental pictures by other thoughts producing disgust and horror of sensuality. The lama focuses all his attention on a certain part of his body and imagines that it becomes ulcerated. The more unpleasant the ulcer looks in the mind of the meditating lama and the more horror the deformity inspires, the better for the success of his profound religious exertions. Then the lama imagines that the ulcer spreads and finally covers all his body, emitting tremendous quantities of pus and blood. If this exercise is carried out in the right way, the lama must actually *believe* that his whole body is ulcerated. He must feel the pain and intense agony of his condition. It may happen that lamas are actually taken ill when indulging in such horrible mental pictures. In some cases the disease may become serious. It has been brought about by sheer auto-suggestion.

After seeing his own body in an ulcerated and horrible state the lama goes a step farther. He imagines the whole world peopled with numerous human beings and his horrible ulcer begins to eat into their bodies as well, until all human beings living in this world become an agonizing concourse of ulcerating and aching bodies.

If the meditating lama has not become ill after all these horrible visions and still has the strength to go on with them, he begins to imagine that the ulcers are eating away the flesh of all human beings living in this world.

These exercises are intended to help the meditating lama to get over the temptations of the flesh and to bring home to him the transient and unreal nature of the pleasures of the senses. They tend to fill the soul of the lama with such horror and disgust with all things mundane that he is bound to become more and more detached from matter and the temptations of the flesh.

One of the meditation exercises of the lamas, however, is more beautiful. It sees the positive side of things and not the negative one. It tends to awaken love and sympathy.

To fight callousness and lack of sympathy with suffering creatures, another type of meditation exercises is taught to the lamas. They are trained to imagine tens of thousands of highly sensitive beings, both men and animals, in the grip of the most horrible pangs. Their bodies writhe with agony and their pitiful cries of pain fill the universe. The lama must actually hear these cries of agony with his "inner ear". These cries become more and more agonizing and swell into a deafening roar of agony.

Then the meditating lama tries to evoke thoughts of sympathy with all those suffering creatures. He must do this so whole-heartedly that tears will come to his eyes. And then he will take—in thought—his tears into the palm of his left hand, bring it near to his heart, and throw them out in the direction of those suffering creatures. His tears will soothe their pain as if by a stroke of magic. But it is like pouring a few drops of water into a house on fire. The lama feels that enormous quantities of tears are required to quench the thirst of all those suffering creatures for a little pity and sympathy. So the meditating lama goes on crying and crying. Tears stream down his face while the vision becomes more intense. Finally his tears rush forth like a streamlet, the streamlet swells into a river, and the river at last becomes as mighty as a flood going out to all those who are in agony.

Although some of these meditation exercises are beautiful, they nevertheless tend to bring about results *by outward practices*. This is contrary to the ways of the real hermits of Tibet. The latter do not use any outward practices to *fight* the symptoms of human imperfection. The hermits go right to the cause. They work *from within*, whereas the meditating lama works *from outside towards the inside*.

Quite unlike the lamas, the hermits do not separate matter and spirit. They try to *spiritualize matter*, whereas the meditating lamas tend to *separate matter and spirit by detaching spirit from matter*.

Life should not be merely material. But life cannot be merely spiritual either. It must be *both*. Just as the ultra-materialistic conception of life, so widely current in the West, tends to detach matter from spirit, thus making life a poor and worthless thing, the meditation exercises of the East make the same mistake in the opposite direction. They tend to cause the meditating person to separate spirit from matter.

If one carefully watches the lamas at times when they do not happen to be meditating to find out how they behave in the little things of their daily lives, one finds that *they are no more humane than others*. Their kindness and sympathy are only accorded on certain occasions. They are not continual, spontaneous, and effortless like the sweet and unofficious kindness of the real Tibetan hermits, who try to understand the full significance of matter and to spiritualize it by realizing its meaning. Only people who understand life, only people who have realized that life is both matter *and* spirit and who continually express this understanding in their daily lives are *really human*.

Humaneness is the thing badly needed in this world, which dies from lack of love. We need people who are humane, really and spontaneously humane, in the little things of their daily lives. We have enough idealists who have occasional fits of idealism and tread the worm on the ground while they are looking for the stars.

There is a story about a Western idealist whom his wife called to the sick bed of her father, asking him to attend to the patient's wishes.

When she returned a few hours later, her father was dead and the idealist was seated in the sick-room making plans for a big idealistic scheme to help the world, in which he, of course, was the central figure. While the "idealist" had been making his great plans he had forgotten all about the dying man who had had nothing to drink and no one else to give him a little attention!

The official medicine of the Tibetans is in the hands of the lamas.

A large number of medicinal plants grow in the south of Tibet in the Himalayan region. They are occasionally used by the lamas for curative purposes, but in most cases the medical methods of the Tibetan doctor seem to be quite ridiculous to Western eyes.

I saw lamas actually spit on wounds or sprinkle water into the faces of their patients, no matter what they happened to suffer from.

Tibetan pharmacology works on principles entirely different from those of the analogous branch of Western science.

What do you think of this Tibetan prescription:

> Take the kidneys from a domestic yak and dip them into blood. Then write with the blood the four holy words on the ground. After this put the kidneys inside a little bag made of sheepskin, sewn up in the moonlight. Fill

the bag with freshly collected dung and close it well. Then go round it seven times, turning your right side to the bag while you are moving. Then open the bag in a pious mood and take out the kidneys. They have now become a patent medicine against almost any disease.

A learned Westerner may laugh at this, but it is a fact that three hundred years ago the cure for rheumatism recognized by Western faculties of medicine was the administration of fat from human corpses. This method of curing rheumatism was considered infallible by the official medical science of the time.

Not very long ago bleeding was considered by Western science a remedy against many complaints. Today we have other "infallible" methods, such as vaccination and the like. But these "infallible" methods will give way to other "infallibilities" once the medical fashion changes. In the long run our scientific methods are subject to fashion just as much as is the feminine sex.

A Tibetan lama preparing his infallible kidney medicine would just as much resent being laughed at as many folk in the West who take themselves very seriously, considering themselves to be strictly in line with the thoughts of their age and environment.

I was greatly struck by the gross ignorance of the Tibetan lamas regarding the most elementary anatomical facts. This seems strange in a country where cutting up human corpses after death is a widespread practice. Many a lama, for instance, imagines that it is the kidneys which supply the seminal liquid and that the spine has a direct anatomical connection with the upper part of the chest! Unless the lamas intend these ideas to be taken symbolically, their ignorance must be appalling.

Tibetan medicine very seldom takes the analytical viewpoint. It does not envisage the various parts of the body as being distinct from others, but deals with the whole body synthetically. The more learned type of Tibetan physiologist, as the hermits told me, speaks of invisible humours which pervade the human body and circulate in it. According to Tibetan scientists, an unbalanced state of those humours—mostly brought about by psychical reactions, or "ghosts" as the Tibetans put it—brings about disease, but they practically never look for a specific *seat* of the disease, and begin to treat the subtle invisible body rather than the gross physical body.

On the whole it would appear that the Tibetans err in the direction diametrically opposed to the cardinal sin of Western medicine, viz. exaggerated specialization and localization. Our medical science, on the whole, does not take things synthetically enough, whereas the medical science of the Tibetans utterly disregards local seats of disease. Maybe the right course lies somewhere half way between the two extremes.

A Westerner trying to use a disinfectant, for example, would be laughed at by Tibetan scientists. The Tibetans say that epidemics are caused by bad thoughts and that good thoughts are a powerful disinfectant.

In their turn people in the West may laugh at this. But Western scientists themselves have ascertained that the water of certain rivers coming from the Himalayan region checks the development of all germs of disease, and many people whom the Tibetans credit with strong powers to emit good thoughts live precisely in that region.

CHAPTER VI

TIBETAN MIRACLES

THE "infallible" medical methods of the professional healers are at the disposal of anyone who is willing to employ their services, which are, of course, rendered against payment in money or in kind. On the other hand, the wise men of Tibet never claim that *their* methods of curing disease are infallible. Nevertheless they do possess methods of curing disease which are almost miraculous in their effects, but, contrary to the habits of the professional healers, these wise men never do anything for the purpose of gaining something, and absolutely refuse to put their marvellous methods of curing disease at the disposal of everybody.

To Western eyes this attitude seems to be rather callous and one has to examine it very closely and with a very broad mind to find an explanation and excuse for it, but let me emphasize the fact that these men who so intensely feel the suffering of others do so in a spirit of sacrifice.

I had my first experience with one of these

wise healers—I had met them before, but had never previously seen them perform a healing operation—in the district of Tokdjalung, when a stone came down from the mountain-side and would have most certainly killed a passing Tibetan had not a young man, with great presence of mind, pushed him aside at the last moment, saving his life. Unluckily the rescuer was so much concerned with saving the stranger's life that in his generous impulse he had forgotten his own safety. A smaller stone which fell immediately after the big one tore savagely down his right arm from shoulder down to wrist, tearing away the skin and inflicting a deep flesh wound at least twenty inches in length.

The poor chap suffered terrible pain as a result and lost so much blood that his clothes were soaked with it down to his knees before any of the bystanders had time to come to his assistance.

No one had anything that could be used as a dressing and I was just about to pull out the package of radio-active earth I carried in the breast-pocket of my Tibetan clothes, intending to smear its contents over the wound and to make some primitive dressing afterwards by tearing up one of my pieces of clothing, when I was stopped by a Tibetan who had witnessed the accident. I immediately noticed the fact that he was scrupulously clean—a very strange phenomenon in Tibet—and his whole bearing was majestic, and yet humble—that strange mixture of conscious power and humility which characterizes all really great men. His face was not young, and yet it was practically without wrinkles. He had beautiful black eyes, and tears of sympathy were streaming down his cheeks.

When he said, "Stop; let me do it," it sounded like a mild entreaty, but the sound of his crystalline voice seemed to go right to the heart.

He went up to this youngster writhing in his agony. He gently touched his hair and cheeks. The blood now streamed down the helper's clothes, but he did not seem to mind this. With infinite tenderness he caressed the young man's head. The pain must have disappeared as if by a stroke of a magic wand. The boy, who had been moaning with pain a few seconds before, looked up and smiled

Then the other seized his arm and made some passes over it. I am unable to say whether he actually touched the bleeding wound or whether his hand passed over it about an inch from it. Be that as it may, the bleeding stopped instantly.

Then the helper tore away a piece from his clean garb which—contrary to the clothes of the other Tibetans—seemed to consist of one single piece of cloth. He made a dressing over the wound. The young man continued to smile. All pain had disappeared as if by magic.

"Now, my dear boy," said the man with the brilliant eyes, "go. If you have good thoughts —and I do not doubt you will have them, you good, kind-hearted creature—your wound will heal in a few days."

"Thank you," stammered the youngster.

"Don't thank me," returned the helper. "Thank yourself. Love has cured you. You have given love and love has helped you. *Live in such a way that I shall never regret having helped you. Kale peb.*"*

These words, uttered with infinite kindness and love, were also a command. Tears of emotion and gratitude streamed down the face of the youngster as he went on his way.

Strange to say, the Tibetans often show tears of joy and pity, but they seldom show tears of pain or express sadness and mental anguish.

The other Tibetans had not uttered a word. They hardly dared to look at the holy man, and when he said "good-bye" to them they moved, trembling and awe-stricken, out of his presence.

---

* Good-bye.

I was the only one who remained on the scene of this almost miraculous healing.

He came a little nearer. His beautiful eyes sparkled. When I looked into them I forgot the past and the future and became intensely conscious of the *present*.

"I should make a good doctor, should I not?" he asked smilingly.

How strange! He exactly expressed the thought that had crossed my mind a few seconds before.

"Yes," I replied. What was the use of posing as a deaf-and-dumb person in the presence of someone who could read other people's thoughts?

"And yet I cure people only in quite exceptional cases," he went on. "Of what use would it be, for instance, if I cured a person who had been taken ill as a result of continual overeating? By the way, people do not overeat themselves in Tibet so often as they do in the West." He gave me a significant glance.

I could not help starting slightly.

"Don't get uneasy," he said, "I shall never give you away. People of my type are not likely to betray anyone."

I felt quite reassured.

"Well," he went on, "I should cure a person taken ill by overeating only in case I felt that he would not begin overeating as soon as he was cured. There are people who would use the help given in such a manner as to become still more harmful to others and still more cruel to their own poor bodies. But," he added, "there are exceptions. I myself have just healed someone. You saw it."

"You helped the youngster," I said. "Would you have helped the man who had been rescued by him?"

"Don't think I am brutal, friend, when I tell you that I should not have helped him."

"Do you mean that?"

"I always mean what I say."

"Isn't that a harsh and unkind attitude?"

"It seems to be if you view things superficially. But in reality it is not. All misfortune that befalls us is of our own making—the result of evil thoughts and evil actions. We reap what we sow. The man for whom the stone was destined was rescued this time, but sooner or later he will be in the same situation. If not in this life then in some future life."

How well I understood this man. Sometimes I did not catch the meaning of more than three or four words in a whole sentence, and yet I understood all that he was saying.

"Shall we not fight evil? Shall we not fight war, for instance," I asked him.

"War is the outcome of evil thoughts, of man's selfishness," he replied. "Many people

TIBETAN MIRACLES 139

are warlike at heart. They fight those around them continually in various ways, and at the same time they talk of peace. If people are against war *because they are afraid of war* their resistance is of no value. Don't let us fight symptoms, but let us change our hearts."

I realized how little chance such a man would have of being understood by most people, in no matter what country.

The kindness of the wise men of Tibet is a kindness of strength. It is impersonal in the widest sense, far-sighted and just, whereas the kindness of the other Tibetans, including also many priests, pilgrims, and so-called idealists, is a kindness born of weakness. It is essentially short-sighted and self-centred and on the whole disastrous in its effects, because it merely *covers up symptoms*, thus making people forget all about the inherently rotten state of affairs, due to a wrong conception of life, which has produced those symptoms.

Compared with the total population of Tibet, which probably amounts to a couple of millions, the number of these wise Tibetans is exceedingly small. It is certainly *much lower* than one thousand.

They are greatly respected by the population, although they never make the slightest effort to become popular. The opinion of other people is quite a negligible matter to the wise men of Tibet, whereas the whole meaningless lives of other Tibetans bear the stamp of other peoples' opinions.

The popularity of the wise men of Tibet is enormous. The very fact of being granted the privilege to talk with them confers a certain distinction in the eyes of the Tibetan masses. As some Tibetans had seen me in conversation with the holy man after curing the youngster, this was likely to give me so much prestige and make me the object of so much attention in the district that the wise man—who, of course, knew that I was a Westerner—advised me to leave the district as quickly as possible, and helped me in every possible way to accomplish this.

However, before parting with him, I asked him:

"Do you think you are great?"

He smiled. "Nothing is high and nothing is low, my friend," he replied. "The insect is just as important as a small man or a so-called great man. There is just as much turmoil in a kettle of water which is boiling up as in the creation and downfall of an empire or the creation or destruction of a universe. All is relative. There is merely the passing and the eternal. What will be left of the bones of the greatest men in six thousand years' time? Not even their memory may survive. All is relative, my friend. I am not greater than the bird in the sky or the worm in the ground. Only life goes on. The form is immaterial."

These men do not want to be respected, and yet they are respected. They are like children at heart, that is to say childlike and simple. They seem to avoid the most dreadful pitfall in the way of a person rising spiritually, namely spiritual arrogance. They are humble servants of humanity without any claim to spiritual rank or distinctions be they ever so subtle.

There are Tibetans who take advantage of the great prestige of the real hermits of Tibet by making an effort to give themselves an outward appearance that is similar, posing as real hermits. Even the lamas often find it useful to pose as hermits in order to heighten their authority. They will retire into solitude for several years and become "hermits" outside the monasteries for the purpose of becoming more respected and gaining promotion to the higher ranks of the Tibetan priesthood.

The careful observer does very well to keep the two types distinct. There is an enormous difference between the real Tibetan hermit and those who merely pose as hermits for selfish purposes. On the whole, the real hermits are far more inaccessible than the hermits of the other kind. They appear only when they positively know that it is of some use to show themselves either, in rare cases, for teaching or to help somebody.

Travellers may visit the most inaccessible parts of Tibet where the hermits really live. They may get to places only a few hundred yards distant from their humble abodes, and yet they will never meet them if the hermits do not wish to show themselves. The real hermits are never out to satisfy people's curiosity. They sometimes give information, but when they do so they always have some constructive purpose in view.

Practically all the so-called hermits of Tibet, who live in small cells hewn in the rock, and who often spend many years in utter darkness, are not genuine hermits. Every day food is brought to these pseudo-hermits and they never see the person bringing it so that their isolation is complete.

It is not necessary for the real hermits to follow any of these outward practices, such as dark cells, to be able to concentrate. If they go into seclusion it is merely for the purpose of avoiding coming into contact with the curious.

However, not all people of the genuine "hermit" type appear in the visible form of hermits. Some of them do not live in seclusion at all and look so like ordinary human beings that they can only be recognized as hermits by other hermits. There is really no *outward sign* by which such people can be recognized. It is a curious fact that occasionally, when he feels the need for doing so, a really wise hermit of Tibet may intentionally adopt filthy habits. He may do it, for instance, for the purpose of curing people of their worship of the visible form of great men.

A small number of people of the genuine "hermit" type even live inside the Tibetan monasteries as lamas. Lamas who have turned religion into business, or who are "spiritual" because they expect some subtle reward for being spiritual, will never realize the real nature of the other type and mission. It is probable that the lama who saved me in the monastery belonged to this category.

The real hermits never make people intentionally afraid, neither do they try to make them believe in their powers; but the false hermits do both. Genuine hermits have nothing to give and nothing to promise. They can only say to people who approach them:

"Look at the world with all its horrible comedies and sufferings, due to human ignorance. People are selfish because they erroneously think that selfishness is necessary for their happiness. All this erroneous seeking of happiness at the expense of suffering inflicted on others leads only to so much anguish and pain that if you could hear at this moment all the cries of agony in the universe you would not be able to stand it, it would sound so heart-rending. And you, my friend—who know all this—can you stand aside and do nothing? Don't alleviate symptoms, but go right to the cause. *Change your heart*, and when your heart is changed, you will live your own teaching and influence the world by your living example."

The genuine hermits thus declare that the impulse to change one's life must come from within. It is wrong to use outward practices to become holy. The latter can only lead to short moments of artificially maintained "holiness" which provides an excuse for continued heartlessness.

"Do you care for money or other possessions?" one of the genuine hermits was asked once in my presence.

"No," he replied.

"Why?"

"I have all I want."

"But how do you get it?"

"Life itself gives to me all that I want."

"But why does life not give all they want to others? There are so many people who are hungry and crave a little food; there are people who badly need money—and yet life does not give it to them."

"Life is just, my friend," the hermit returned. "If life does not give you something life knows that you would misuse it or that you need suffering for the moment. The greatest catastrophe that could come to most people would be the instant satisfaction of all their desires, because they desire things for their little selves, and not for life as a whole."

The real hermits of Tibet eat very little. Yet they declare that they never make an *effort* to abstain from food. They say they do not fast merely because they expect to get something for fasting in the form of a material or spiritual reward. They seem to be so spiritual *from within* that they are seldom hungry.

One day I bluntly asked a Tibetan hermit how he had learned to read people's thoughts.

"I never began to make an effort to pry into other people's thoughts," he answered. "It all came on by itself. I broke down my self-centredness, and when I reached *from within* into a state of consciousness *which would never permit me to take advantage of my capacity to read other people's thoughts, I could read them.* But I never developed this faculty by exercises of one kind or another."

"Many people would like to be able to read other people's thoughts," I remarked.

"Yes," he replied, "and if egocentrical people could penetrate into the private thoughts of others the world would become still more terrible than it is at present. It could be like living in a city where all the walls and partitions in the houses were made of glass. This would only be possible in a world where people were unselfish even to the point of voluntarily abstaining from taking an idle interest in other people's affairs."

"I sometimes feel people's thoughts myself," I told the hermit, "and I know it is no pleasant feeling."

"If thought-reading stimulates sympathy with the troubles of others, it is all right," he replied, "but woe if it merely stimulates contempt. And where thought-reading is developed by outer practices it usually leads to the latter. If thought-reading comes to you *from within* because you love others so deeply that you feel one with them, it leads to the former and then there is no danger that you will use this faculty for selfish purposes.

"And mind," he added, "the word selfish is used here in the widest sense. Even if that faculty was used only for self-protection and self-defence it would be wrong. Superphysical faculties must not be used for physical purposes. That would be a crime.

"The greater a man's power and understanding in the spiritual realm, the greater his responsibilities. As his powers increase there must be a corresponding increase in love and compassion and the latter must come spontaneously from within."

The sex-life of the Tibetan hermits bears the stamp of abstemiousness. Many of them do not seem to have any sex-life at all. Other hermits seem to have reduced indulgence to an incredibly low minimum corresponding, as one of them told me, to the number of contacts of an animal living in perfect freedom, viz. about twice a year.

The highest form of cosmical energy used by a great poet or great composer for creating things bearing the stamp of the eternal is essentially the same energy as the one used in sex matters. A real saint employs his creative energies in such a way that they are used creatively, thus leaving little or nothing for sexual use. But the false saint does not direct these forces correctly. Not being creative he has a strong sexual appetite, the phenomena of which he regards as temptation, and accordingly he works hard to suppress them out of fear and selfishness.

Real Tibetan saints are moral because they

want to be moral and their non-indulgence is natural and effortless. But the "virtue" of the so-called saints is strained and artificial. They are virtuous because their so-called virtue gives them advantages, be they only advantages of a subtle kind, such as of imagining themselves seated on a kind of throne and looking down on the "sinner", which may give them—if I may say so—some sort of perverse enjoyment compensating them for their "virtue".

There is a distinct difference between the natural and effortless abstemiousness of a real saint and the artificially subdued sensuality of a so-called saint who is "holy" for selfish reasons. The number of real saints is infinitely smaller than the number of the latter.

In some of the Tibetan monasteries the monks are made to wear cleverly designed appliances destined to cripple certain parts of their body and to force them to be "moral" by depriving them of the physical possibility of being immoral. Such "holiness" is of course grotesque, but many other types of enforced holiness, brought about by fear and constraint, really amount to the same thing although less brutal in appearance.

How light and shade are interwoven and how difficult it is to see realities through the illusion of appearance! An action may have exactly the same aspect—fast, non-indulgence, kindness, etc.

—and yet the most important thing about it, the *motive*, may be different. Very often a brutal and a saintly act have precisely the same physical aspect. And yet so many people who call themselves "spiritual" do not hesitate to judge other people's actions!

The real Tibetan hermits do not judge others, but the false saints never miss a chance to do so. This judging of other people's actions is an excellent touch-stone of real and false spirituality. How do many people who call themselves "spiritual" pass this test?

In a book which is so often read and yet so seldom applied in the little things of our daily lives, it is written "do not judge". We do not know the most important thing about other people's actions: their *motives*. So don't let us judge others. Let us judge *ourselves*. We do know the motives of our *own* actions, and *this* judging is very necessary and useful.

It is stupid to condemn others. Most bad actions are due to ignorance and not to actual malice. If the world is not better than it is, it is our own fault because we have not influenced it sufficiently by example.

"A man's example is more important than his teaching. We must live our own teaching." This is an utterance giving in a few words the attitude of the real Tibetan hermits.

The real hermits have very few actual pupils, and in some cases none at all, but the so-called hermits never can have pupils enough. The latter insist on elaborate ceremonies and solemn greetings whenever they are approached by their pupils. They like to emphasize their dignity and authority by outward marks of respect. The real hermits make light of everything that is strained or artificial. And yet their attitude is commanding. It bears the stamp of the effortless majesty of those who are really great, who do not care what they look like, but only what they *are*. It is said sometimes that no one is great in the eyes of his valet. Well, I wonder what pitiful sort of greatness such a saying must imply. The more one knows the real Tibetan hermits in the little things of their daily lives, the more one respects them. It is the type of respect that is well deserved and not merely demanded.

The authority of the false hermits is elaborately maintained. They calculate the effect of everything they are doing. The real hermits do not do this.

The former often teach their pupils how they can remain warm when sitting out in the bitterly cold Tibetan night. They teach them outward practices to accomplish this end.

The resistance of Tibetan hermits to the

effects of cold is remarkable. Although sometimes they are practically naked—and even if they wear clothes, they are not made of wool—I never saw a fire in their abodes. Even in summer, the Tibetan nights are bitterly cold, the temperature falling below freezing-point.

I have seen them sit motionless for many hours in bitterly cold weather. They do not seem to suffer in the least from the effects of cold, and one may examine their bodies in vain for any visible traces of exposure to cold weather.

Why do they not freeze to death? What is the secret of their perfect resistance to cold?

I often slept in an unheated tent at extremely low temperatures and know by experience that one suffers less from the effects of extremely cold weather when one is relaxed. I often go about in Lapland without putting on a hat at temperatures ranging from 20 to 30 degrees Centigrade under zero, without showing any signs of exposure to cold afterwards.

Relaxation seems to be the essential thing to acquire immunity from the effects of cold. However, it is impossible to teach anybody by exercises how to bring about safely a state of absolute relaxation, for a state of *physical* relaxation *must be the result of a state of psychical relaxation.*

The less one takes an egocentrical view of

life, the less one divides everything in life into the "I" and the "non-I", the more one is relaxed psychically, and then physical relaxation automatically follows. The more egocentrical we are, the more we keep soul and body in a state of tension. If we take life in terms of *having* instead of in terms of *being*, the perpetual state of wanting to gain something puts us into a state of cramp, both psychically and physically.

The real Tibetan saints do not want to have *anything*. They take life in terms of *being*, not in terms of *having*.

If you watch a beautiful sunset or listen to wonderful music and entirely forget that you are Mr. or Mrs. So-and-So, you do not desire anything for Mr. or Mrs. So-and-So, and in those moments you feel the bliss of the impersonal. You do not want to *have* the sunset for yourself and deprive others of it, you do not want to *possess* that beautiful music, and yet you feel happy and know the bliss of absolute unselfishness which seeks no reward *whatever* for being unselfish. That is *real* spirituality.

And if you hold on to that conception of life, even during the turmoils and hardships of everyday life, you live the life of the real saints, those simple and really *human* beings with whom religion is a living thing, and not merely lip-service or theory.

The remarkable resistance to cold of the real saints of Tibet, therefore, is a *consequence* of a perfect psychical and physical relaxation due to their non-egocentrical conception of life.

And how about the others, the *so-called* saints?

They know that cold weather has no grip on the real saints and try to ape them, as they know that it is advantageous to conquer the effects of cold in order to impress others with their powers. They therefore endeavour to bring about a state of relaxation by certain practices coupled with psychical exertions.

In both cases the result is quite extraordinary, and the mastery over the effects of cold is complete.

Dangerous as the practices of the so-called saints are to the Tibetans, they are all the more dangerous for Westerners, whose nervous system is much more likely to be wrecked by them than the Tibetans'.

The nervous system of the Tibetans has, no doubt, acquired a certain resistance to the harmful effects of these practices, since these things have been practised there for generations. The nervous system of the white man is much more exposed to them by the absence of this gradual hereditary adaptation. Moreover, the strenuous life of the West puts in itself a very heavy burden on the nervous resistance of the white man, who would be very ill-advised to expose himself to an additional terrible strain on his nerves. I do not doubt that any egocentrical white person trying to carry out these practices would sooner or later destroy himself, and as to the few non-egocentrical people, there is no need for them to practise at all.

The real saints seem to be able to master the forces of Nature, although they never make a show of possessing these powers. They would never make a demonstration of them simply for the purpose of convincing the sceptical, or in order to satisfy mere curiosity. Moreover, I have good reasons to believe that they would not even use these powers in self-defence. Also, their faculty of perfect penetration of other people's thoughts, of which I had evidence again and again when coming into contact with them in Tibet, is never made use of by them for selfish purposes, and when I say so I give the word "selfishness" its widest possible meaning. I do not doubt that had the false saints possessed the faculty of reading my thoughts, they would not have hesitated a moment to give me away to the lamas.

These false saints manage sometimes to rule over the forces of Nature to a slight degree, but in nearly all cases the work done for this purpose is so harmful to them and exhausts them so terribly that they work their miracles as seldom as possible, and whenever they have a chance to do so they replace them by some cleverly staged music-hall trick. There are, undoubtedly, some genuine psychical phenomena in Tibet, but they are few and far between, and a tremendous number of alleged cases of phenomena have to be examined before a genuine one, which baffles the most sceptical observer, can be discovered. People who imagine that the flying lamas are numerous in Tibet are mistaken. On an average, one must keep one's eyes wide open for many weeks before one meets even one flying lama, and then the phenomenon usually is far too rapid to permit of lengthy observation.

I saw flying lamas only on two occasions. The nearest distance between the *lung-gom-pa* and myself was about forty yards on one occasion and only eight to ten yards on the other. In both cases the phenomenon presented almost the same aspect. The hands and feet of the lamas swung to and fro like a pendulum. The speed at which they progressed was amazing, and in the case in which the lama was only about ten yards distant, the glimpse I got of him was sufficient to enable me to ascertain that *he was not out of breath*. I had the impression that he was in a state of trance, his face looking somewhat like the face of one of the genuine Western mediums—probably we only have about thirty good mediums in Europe and America put together—but I could not help feeling that the Lama was more positive and conscious in his state of trance than are Western mediums. Judging by careful examination of the foot-prints, the weight of his body must have been diminished to some extent, although I should not like to give an estimate. My camera had been destroyed by robbers, and even had I still been able to use it, the light would not have been good enough to have taken a photograph of a person moving at a speed of at least fifteen miles an hour. On the second occasion on which I met a flying lama, the light was good for taking a snapshot at about one or two hundredths of a second, but I was not alone to watch the phenomenon, so even had my camera still been good enough for use, it would have been impossible to have taken a photograph without arousing the curiosity and suspicion of the Tibetans.

I had no occasion to regret the destruction of my camera, anyhow, because I know by actual experience that photographic evidence of psychical phenomena is very seldom of much use.

TIBETAN MIRACLES 157

Many years ago I took a delight in securing genuine ghost pictures taken at seances in the West. I then made an equal number of faked ghost pictures by taking three or four photographs on the same plate. My next action was to mix the two sets of ghost photographs, which I handed to people who had had great practical experience in judging psychical phenomena, requesting them to find the genuine ghost photograph amongst the faked ones. They failed miserably. They pronounced many faked photographs to be genuine, and pronounced about just as many genuine ghost pictures to be faked ones!

The testing of psychical phenomena by suitable apparatus is a much more reliable way of ascertaining their reality. The explorer travelling in disguise is handicapped by the impossibility of using instruments designed for the purpose of psychical research. I have given lectures on the psychical phenomena of Tibet for the members of various Societies of Psychical Research in Scandinavia, Holland, and other countries, and after my lectures I was always willing to answer questions about the minutest details of my experiences in Tibet. Nevertheless, when the facts about psychical phenomena are presented for examination, we must not lose sight of the fact that even in Western countries, where considerable facilities exist for carrying out research work of this kind, the greatest brains of this age are still at variance as to whether the evidence concerning the reality of psychical phenomena shall be admitted or not.

Personally, I am inclined to believe that if an individual concentrates all his will-power—and energies, during a period of say twenty years—on the task of producing a particular occult phenomenon, such as levitating himself a few feet into the air, he may succeed, although he may have to pay dearly for the accomplishment by gradually ruining his health and nervous balance. But in order to bring about such a result, I do not think that, say, half an hour's work per day during twenty years will be sufficient. He must really concentrate all his energies, all his will-power, and all his time to that end.

And if a person who happens to be self-centred finally succeeds in going up into the air, I think the ultimate punishment for this selfish dabbling in occultism will be—self-destruction.

The dark occultists of Tibet, viz. people who engage themselves in the dangerous practice of using occult powers for selfish purposes, inspire the Tibetans with fear and horror. The most powerful of them are supposed by the

Tibetans to possess the dark power to kill people at a distance of many hundred yards, by sending them a kind of subtle invisible arrow made of the fine substance of which the subtle invisible body (see Chapter V) consists. This may, of course, be gross exaggeration, but it seems to be beyond doubt that these men can work harm if they choose to do so. However, they must be very careful in the choice of their victims, for it is a fact recognized by all occultists that an absolutely unselfish and fearless man cannot be hurt by adverse influences, and that any hostile influence destined to work harm to him automatically bounces back and injures the person trying to harm him. He would act like a man throwing a ball against a wall for the purpose of damaging it, and receiving it back on his nose.

Some of the false saints of Tibet succeed in developing clairvoyance and clairaudience to a very slight degree, but the real hermits possess these powers in an extraordinary way. Fairly often I passed false saints in Tibet, none of whom ever knew the fact that I was not a Tibetan. On two or three occasions only they seemed to feel vaguely that there was something unusual about me.

The belief in the existence of the aura, the invisible cloud surrounding our dense physical bodies, is fairly general in Tibet. The aura is said to be visible only to clairvoyants. "Visible" is not the right term though. The clairvoyant senses the aura. In most cases he does not *see* it, but *perceives* it with his or her whole ethereal body.

It is difficult to transcribe the experiences of a clairvoyant into a language made for describing physical things. Supposing a normal person tried to describe to an audience of blind people what yellow, red, or blue are like! His description would be just as inadequate as the terms used by a clairvoyant in describing a thing his audience had never experienced.

It is, naturally, simple to dispose of the whole problem of clairvoyance by declaring that it is all humbug. I do not think such a simple and convenient way of dealing with unwelcome facts is justified, for sometimes when a person visits various clairvoyants who do not know each other and who live in different districts, they will give descriptions of his aura which tally closely.

There *are* genuine clairvoyants in Tibet, but they do not seem to be very numerous. False clairvoyants, on the other hand, abound. Every lama of high rank, for instance, is credited with the power of clairvoyance, and most of the older lamas try to make people believe that they are clairvoyants, in order to heighten their authority.

When coming in contact with the type of individual in Tibet who feels that he absolutely needs a miracle in order to facilitate his spiritual business, explorers must be on their guard. There are cases where Tibetan "sorcerers" do not seem to hesitate to use hypnotic powers in order to make their audience "see" things which do not exist. Great care also from this angle is necessary, therefore, in judging alleged Tibetan miracles. Whenever possible, material traces—be they ever so slight—should be examined after a phenomenon has taken place. The author avoided mixing in with a crowd when studying such phenomena wherever, of course, this was possible without attracting attention. Even if there may be no conscious hypnotic influence present, it is not a good thing to mix with crowds. People anxious to maintain an independent and objective attitude should give them a wide berth.

However, even if all these reserves and exceptions to the reality of Tibetan phenomena are taken into consideration, the absolute reality of thought-transmission over fairly long distances and certain other less striking phenomena, such as psychometry and the like, is unquestionable.

Many of my readers will be surprised to learn that sometimes phenomena which can be produced at an altitude of 10,000 feet do not come off at an altitude of 13,000 feet. There are phenomena which can be produced in clear weather only, and a subsequent change in weather conditions entirely paralyses the "sorcerer". Does not this go to show that these "miracles" are subject to well-established laws of Nature, and that there is nothing really miraculous about them?

In one instance it was quite obvious that psychometrical faculties were greatly disturbed by rainy weather. I had wrapped up various small items in a cloth and showed the parcel to a Tibetan reputed for his powers of psychometry. He could always tell me, at least approximately, what the cloth contained without opening the parcel. On one occasion I had placed an animal's tooth within it. When I asked him to tell me what was hidden there, his answer was:

"Something that hurts!"

His answer was correct, although not correct to the letter. Many answers are similarly vague.

A subsequent change in the weather paralysed his psychometrical faculty entirely, and he did not regain it until the weather had changed back again.

Even under the most favourable conditions the judging of psychical phenomena is a difficult matter. Answers are often only nearly right. Furthermore, the fact that someone watches the phenomenon with hostile scepticism may paralyse the whole affair, and nothing will happen. Many people judge psychical phenomena like a judge who has his sentence ready before a trial. They watch phenomena with the judgment "humbug" already well-established in their minds. As a well-known scientist once told me: "They do not wish to admit a thing which they fail to understand." Scepticism is a very good and necessary thing when judging psychical phenomena, but *hostile* scepticism goes much too far.

Not only some of the so-called hermits in Tibet occasionally produce miracles—in quite exceptional cases, apparently genuine ones, in most cases faked ones—but also, some of the lamas in the monasteries. Especially with the latter the few seemingly genuine phenomena are literally swamped with an enormous quantity of music-hall tricks, and sometimes the grossest types of fraud.

There is a venerable priest, for instance, who makes his pupils go about announcing that he can go up into the air at will by reducing to naught the weight of his venerable body. Many hundreds of enthusiasts go every day to watch the phenomenon. Is it not nice and refreshing to see a holy man go up several times into the air and come back to the ground immediately afterwards?

The curious crowds, worked up into a state of pious sheepishness, gather round a carefully closed cell. They cannot see what is going on within, but from time to time they *hear* the impact of a human body falling back to the ground. In the eyes of the Tibetan crowd this is conclusive evidence of the reality of the phenomenon. They believe in the miracle, and afterwards are as generous as possible in their contributions towards the living expenses of the lama and his pupils. Their childlike credulity is, perhaps, coupled with a certain amount of fear of so powerful a man, to whom even the forces of Nature are assumed to render obedience.

A civilized Westerner may smile at this. But too often Westerners, when they are crowded together, are not more critical than Tibetan crowds.

In some cases the Tibetan priests do not hesitate to eke out their incomes by selling "miracle" shoes alleged to carry the person wearing them over rivers and lakes, by preventing them from sinking.

These shoes are like ordinary Tibetan felt shoes, but with one difference, they are exceedingly expensive. Intending buyers are informed that the sale of the shoes is subject to two conditions. Firstly, the purchase-price has to be paid before the shoes are tried, and secondly, the miracle shoes must be tested alone, in the absence of witnesses.

Just when a lama happened to be selling miracle shoes to a crowd of credulous Tibetans, five or six people, who had bought miracle shoes a few hours earlier, returned, in order to protest, as they had found the shoes useless. They had tried to walk on the surface of water with disastrous results. "*Rimpotshé*,"* said one of them to the lama in the presence of the crowd, "you sold me this pair of miracle shoes, and I carefully complied with your instructions. I paid the price in advance and no one else was present when I tried them.

"And now I come back to protest," he continued, "as the shoes failed to work and are of no use at all."

One should have expected the pious lama to be greatly embarrassed on hearing this protest in the presence of a large crowd, but he was quite unperturbed.

---

* Holy father.

"Did you really sink in, friend?" he asked mildly.

"Yes," replied the Tibetan, "and I was nearly drowned. I went down in the water as quickly as a person wearing ordinary shoes."

A murmur went through the crowd. The lama raised his voice.

"I shall tell you why these shoes are of no use to you," he said. "The miracle shoes are holy, and if *sinners* wear them, they lose their magical powers. I always walk with them on the surface of rivers and lakes if no witnesses are present, and if another person who is not too bad a sinner complies with my instructions and tries them out alone, they always work."

The Tibetan was greatly humiliated on being called a bad sinner in the presence of the large crowd, and the lama went on, speaking louder and louder, presenting the poor chap to the crowd as a living example of a man leading a sinful life. It was not long before this Tibetan, who had boldly stepped forward to protest, literally took to his heels, accompanied by a few other Tibetans who had also returned to protest. They all ran away, and the pious lama quietly continued his business.

The greater the quackery in a Tibetan monastery, the larger the crowd. One cannot help thinking, therefore, that most Tibetans like to be cheated, and that they create the quacks by the desire of the individual to be cheated.

Perhaps this is why the wise men of Tibet do not succeed in changing Tibet.

CHAPTER VII

ETERNAL YOUTH

THERE is nothing more wonderful than youth, youthful enthusiasm, the capacity to feel deeply and to experience the profound ecstasy of life. Is it inevitable that we must lose this glorious thing, youth, slowly and inexorably?

The art of keeping young is quite a different matter to merely lengthening our lives.

At the time of the Thirty Years' War, when whole countries in Europe lost about half their population by war, famine, and pestilence, the average lifetime of man was—*ten years*. Last century it was *thirty* to *forty years*. Today it is nearly *sixty years*, and serious scientists speak of the possibility of lengthening, very soon, the average lifetime of humanity to *eighty years*.

Hélas! all this progress is more apparent than real. The statistics do not state at what age man begins to be *old*. Man living say 300 years ago probably kept young longer than our contemporaries.

In this world of ready-made pleasures and tonics, in this world of so-called "intense" life which in most cases is nothing more than the seeking of speed and sensation in order to forget one's own terrible emptiness and unhappiness, men and women age far too quickly. Most people get old and disillusioned very early. Even if life itself does not flee, the greatest thing on earth, Youth, is rapidly lost.

The masses in Tibet make other mistakes, mostly of a "spiritual" nature, and they also age prematurely, but the real Tibetan hermits manage to remain young almost indefinitely. There are rumours in Tibet that some of these men are five or six hundred years old, but such stories may be true or they may not be true. It is impossible to prove a man's age once he is supposed to be several hundred years old, since he outlives all witnesses.

However, some of these men, who look like healthy men of about thirty-five years of age, must be at least one hundred years old, as very many old people living in the same districts have seen these men during fifty or sixty years or more and declare they have not changed their appearance during this period and that they certainly have not grown older.

What is the secret of their practically everlasting youth?

The best opportunity of studying such a man was offered to me when I stayed for five days in the abode of a brother of one of my best friends in Tibet. Both are hermits who seem to possess the power to maintain themselves young almost indefinitely. One of them lives south of the Gobi desert. Incidentally, it was this man who procured me Tibetan clothes and greatly improved my accent by marvellous pronunciation exercises. His brother lives in Southwestern Tibet, and it was the latter who offered me hospitality in his abode.

These hermits do not share the view, so common amongst the so-called saints of Tibet, that dirt is a sign of holiness. They are just as clean outwardly as they are inwardly. Their clothes are neither rich nor excessively shabby. Only a few of them are exceptionally tall, and although they eat very little—and in fine and clear weather, sometimes nothing at all—they are not very thin. It must be admitted, however, that they do not seem to carry a single grain of fat.

There was a wonderful atmosphere of serenity in my Tibetan friend's abode. There was a marvellous atmosphere of real hospitality— hospitality so natural and effortless that one felt at home at once.

For three days after I arrived he had hardly eaten anything, and I had began to wonder whether it was his fast which kept him so young. He looked like a man of about thirty, and he sometimes behaved like a boy. Also, his eyes were more the eyes of a boy than those of a fully grown man. His real age—judging from the reliable statements of numerous old people who had seen him many decades ago—must have been ninety years *at least*.

There was nothing solemn and awe-inspiring about him, and one morning when we jokingly pushed each other about to get some exercise, I clasped his body. It was elastic and lithe, like the body of a boy of nineteen.

Again, I wondered whether his eating so little had something to do with his youthful appearance. I just thought this, without asking him. He smiled, looked at me fully with his brilliant eyes, which continually changed their expression, and said :

"It is not fasting that keeps me young, my friend."

"Why do you eat so little, then ?" I asked.

"Because I am practically never hungry," he answered.

"Now, listen very carefully," he went on, after a slight pause. "The moment you make an *effort* to remain young, you get older. *The very moment you make an effort to keep something, you are afraid to lose it.* And *fear poisons a man*, no matter what he does or what he eats. It is fear that destroys people's youth."

"Don't forget that all in life is relative, and that there are *no absolute values*. Even good or evil do not really exist. Nothing is really good or really bad. It all depends on how we use a thing. You can't keep young by certain practices. If we are old *at heart*, physical old age quickly follows, no matter what we eat or what we do to keep young. *And what is youth?* It is *freedom from prejudice, freedom from habitual ways of thinking and habitual ways of living.* So long as we are *spontaneous, loving, and enthusiastic* we are young.

"This is very simple," I ventured to remark. "But most people would like a miraculous liquid giving them everlasting youth."

"Precisely," he replied, "but such a thing as an elixir giving eternal youth does not exist.

"Do not think I am brutal when I show you the world as it really is. If we gave the world an elixir of eternal youth we should only make things worse. Many people use their lives to work harm to others while making now and then a short effort to be good, thus having an excuse for being mischievous all the rest of the time. And how about the unemployment problem?" he added with a significant wink, showing that he knew more about the West than I had imagined. "And how about the problem of overpopulation?" His voice became infinitely sad.

"In a world where man is the enemy of man, a lengthened life only creates additional disorder. Lengthening people's lives *without changing their hearts* would only increase the disorder and suffering in the world. All the troubles of the world are caused by the erroneous attitude of the individual who seeks his own happiness at the expense of the happiness of others. By merely fighting the *symptoms* of that trouble—which include premature old age—we do not make things better. We have fought the symptoms of selfishness for centuries past, and in spite of this the world has become more and more unhappy."

"Are you happy?" I asked.

Tears streamed down his face while he made his answer. "No, I am not. People of my type are often heartbreakingly lonely, if you look at it from a purely human angle. I love others, and yet I feel how infinitely little I can do for them. There is deep tragedy in this. I cannot be happy before the whole world is happy, and there is a long calvary, an infinitely long calvary, still ahead of us before that goal is reached."

I suddenly could not help thinking of a conversation I once had with a learned theologian with whom I had discussed the pleasures of paradise and the sufferings of the damned.

He had seemed to feel that one should not bother much about hell once one is certain that one gets to paradise oneself. But to revert to my conversation.

"Is life worth living?" I asked the hermit.

"Yes," he replied "Life is great Life is glorious, there is always that alternative between vertiginous summits and dreadful chasms. All is relative and there is no certainty. If you realize this you can live with the heart of a boy. Only if you live with the heart of a boy is life worth living. Then you know many things and yet you do not feel superior. I do not think I am an exceptional individual; I am just a humble servant of humanity. I live and love."

"What can we do for the world?" I asked.

"We can be signposts, showing the way to those groping in the darkness. But woe to them if they begin to worship us. *If people wait for signposts to help them, signposts become the greatest hindrance.*"

"But how shall we begin to influence others practically?"

"Most people contribute in some way or other to the sufferings of the world—often without even knowing it themselves," he replied. "All a sincere man can do is not to co-operate with anything he considers stupid, no matter what may be the result for his life and property." He suddenly began to laugh like a naughty boy, his outburst of boyish vivacity strangely contrasting with his serious manner a few moments before. "I must laugh," he said, "when using the word 'property', for I have no property. I have nothing, so I am not afraid to lose anything."

"Shall we recommend people to seek poverty?" I asked.

"No. There is no harm in riches if people do not cling to them."

"So that contempt of money, riches, and power need not be a first step?"

"No. It comes by itself, once people have understood life."

"What should be the first step, then?"

"Understand one's self. It is much easier to understand others than it is to understand ourselves. Don't you think that it is easier for a person to understand the child of someone else, than it is to understand his own child? The more prejudiced and selfishly interested in a thing we are, the more difficult it is to understand. Is there anything which is more difficult to judge objectively than our selves? Tell people to become fully aware of themselves. Tell them to inquire continually into their own motives, to be brutally open to themselves.

That may provide the first incentive to the realization of one's own insufficiencies and thus a first step towards understanding.

"After all, it is very simple. Love! Love more and more intensely! And if your love is free from the poison of ego-centricism you will not feel superior because you have a deeper understanding. If real love begets understanding, this understanding will be free from the dreadful pitfall of spiritual arrogance."

My wise friend did everything himself. Mealtime had come, and he prepared our food. I had a little barley meal with some dried radishes, whereas his meal consisted of perhaps two or three teaspoonfuls of a mixture of herbs that one of his friends had brought down for him from the Himalayas.

"I received a little bag of these three months ago," he said. "There is still much left in it."

"Few Westerners would be content with a meal like this," I observed.

"I do not suggest for a moment that they should eat such food. There is much good in all the progress of civilization," he returned, "but people make a mess out of it. The more they invent machinery, the more they complicate life. So in the end they are none the better for it.

"I should not mind using some Western

machinery up here," he added. "Why should I work an hour a day for a month on my clothes if the same work can be done by a machine in ten minutes?"

"Well, why don't you get one?" I asked.

"I should become too conspicuous up here if I used machinery," he answered, "and then I should hasten the progress of Western penetration here in Tibet, which has already started near the borders of the country, and also in some parts of the Lhasa district."

"Have you a connection with the Lhasa district?" I asked, rather surprised. "I thought this district was one of the most isolated in Tibet."

"Never mind how I get my information," he replied meaningly. "If you go to the Lhasa district yourself, you may check up whether I am right.

"But you cannot go there on this trip. It would not be safe, for you would have to travel in disguise in a district where many white people have already been seen by the inhabitants."

"Perhaps I shall go there on my next visit to Tibet in five or six years," I said.

"Don't be so rash as to make plans, friend," he said. "There may be gigantic upheavals interfering with your plans, although nothing is definitely determined as yet. It all depends on what every one of us is doing. One good thought may pull down the scales in the right direction."

"Why do you not wish Western progress to come to Tibet?" I asked.

"The West makes the horrible mistake of over-emphasizing the importance of matter. This part of the world makes the opposite mistake. Tibet runs away from the material aspect. By bringing machinery up here we should make the pendulum swing in the opposite direction, and the people inevitably would become materialists.

"A new conception of life is necessary all over the world," he went on more loudly; it was as though he had forgotten all about me and spoke to humanity as a whole. "The West runs away from Spirit and the East runs away from Matter. The few people in the West who make an effort to be religious are just like the common folk in the East, they run away from Matter, too. And the few people in the East who, by an effort, break away from what they call religion become materialists like most Western people.

"Unless we create a new conception of life," he went on, "both the East and the West are doomed. We need a new type of humanity which is both Matter and Spirit. Only such people can be *human*. A person running away either from Matter or from Spirit, never is."

He led me to the door of his abode. A glorious landscape lay before our eyes. The air was as clear as crystal. At a distance of about eight English miles, about 2500 feet below us, there was a mountain-lake.

My Tibetan friend showed me an island in the lake. He said that Tibetan hermits lived on the island, and the population considered it their duty to bring food to them. All the winter the lake was frozen until late in the spring, and the food supply was very easy to obtain until then. But when the summer came on rafts could not at first be used, while the ice was melting, as Tibetan rafts consist of blown-up bags made of hides.

Then people risk their lives to bring food to the hermits by walking over the surface of the melting ice. The so-called hermits consider their prayers more effective on the island than elsewhere, and do not want to pray elsewhere, even at the cost of endangering other people's lives.

"Here you see an example of people running away from Matter," my friend said. "They pray, and are good while they pray, but they are not good in their daily lives. Can you imagine a really *humane* being praying on an island, and by doing so, forcing other people to risk their lives when walking over the ice?

"Beware of people who think they are good, my friend," he added. "In most cases we are worst when we imagine we are good."

I had to think of cruel idealists and the wars of Religion. I had to think of the fact that for centuries past a large number of various systems have been established for helping others and for making others better, and that in spite of this the world seems to be a veritable lunatic asylum of stupidities and horrible suffering.

Many of us try to be "good", but often we are good only for a few minutes now and then, and our ideals and short moments of kindness and benevolence only provide us with an excuse for being hypocritical egotists all the rest of our time. Many of us are idealists because it pays to be idealists. Such idealism has no value at all. On the contrary, it helps to cover up symptoms, thus preventing the world from seeing the underlying causes of our troubles.

Let us fight selfishness and imperfection in *ourselves* and not in others. The world would be much better and much more human if people devoted to judging *themselves* only a tenth part of the energies they waste on judging others in thought, words, or action.

Unlike most other Tibetans who begin to

discover how they should live only when their lives are nearly gone, the real Tibetan hermits have the courage to live their own lives undisturbed by habits and prejudices. They are always in love with life while they live. Their outlook on life is a living and dynamic reality.

They do not wish *anything*, not even a long life or health or happiness. They just live without crippling their lives or allowing them to be crippled by others, which attitude requires a good deal of determination in this world. They treat everything kindly—although occasionally they may be harsh to individuals when they think life as a whole demands it—and this "everything" also includes their own bodies. They never ill-treat them. They do not desire anything, and yet everything is given to them.

Strangely enough, their not desiring anything seems to be coupled with an unflinching will-power, but this will-power is never used from the point of view of the "I", but always from the point of view of *everything* which also includes the "I".

They are very wise, probably just because of the fact that they do not accumulate learning like a miser who accumulates gold. They do not judge things with the brain only, but with the brain *and* the heart. And that is wisdom—

namely, not merely the accumulating and cataloguing of innumerable details, but the grasping of vital connections. Someone killing specimens of all unknown species of animals in Tibet, for instance, and examining them very thoroughly, would not be any the wiser for it.

Has our civilization, with all its learning and ever-increasing technical improvements and facilities made us wise and happy? Has our enormous knowledge and information made us wiser than those Tibetan hermits? Certainly not. For we have merely accumulated learning and lack the wisdom to put all this learning and all these improvements to good and constructive purposes.

Even the common Tibetan folk in parts of Tibet, where information about the West is available, do not want Western civilization.

"It brings only unhappiness and strife," they say. "It is not wanted here."

Shall we destroy civilization and climb the trees because we are not wise enough to use it as it ought to be used? If the heart of man changes, civilization will cease to defeat its own purpose. After all, is civilization good or bad? *Nothing* is good or bad. It all depends on how we use it.

The technical and scientific aspect of civilization has progressed at a stupendous rate, but during these times of rapid material progress the heart of man has hardly changed, in spite of whole centuries of talking about love and brotherhood. Is there really a difference between the man who went to the circus 1800 years ago to see people torn to pieces by lions, and the modern man who goes to the circus when there is the prospect of an acrobat breaking his neck?

All Tibetan sellers of spiritual drugs encourage the belief that if one gets near a very saintly person, the very fact of proximity will help one automatically, and will be of spiritual benefit.

In the realm of real spirituality there can be no "advantage". Even the presence of a great and dynamic being does not automatically help one. It merely sets loose everything that is hidden in us, and not only our light sides, but also the other ones. Small wonder that the real hermits are so reluctant to meet the curious multitude.

The real hermits never call themselves "saints". Beware of people who make such an effort to convince you that they are good or moral. If someone really is virtuous, he need not emphasize the fact.

Only once I asked a Tibetan saint whether he was virtuous. His answer was—a merry laugh! And yet I am convinced that he never sinned. The guiding principle of his life was *love*. He never did to others what he didn't want others to do to him. That was his moral code, he told me afterwards.

This hermit who, of course, also knew that I was a white person, gave me answers to very vital questions.

"Tell me whether you have found Reality," I asked him.

"Reality, Truth, Life, God, Eternity, all-embracing Love—all these are one and the same thing," he answered. "You cannot *find* truth. The moment you have *your* truth, it is no longer truth.

"As long as we live we must *seek*," he went on. "Life would have no meaning if there was anything *certain*. The more you are pushed about by life, the better. Never be satisfied, especially with *yourself*."

"Is there no guiding principle?" I asked.

"There is one," he said, while his eyes lit up with infinite love and compassion, "the guiding principle should be Love. If you are true to it, it shows the right way."

We had come up from the valley where I had crossed the river on my floating device just before meeting him. After answering my last question, he increased his speed. So did I. I can walk at six miles an hour without running. But the Tibetan walked faster still!

"Are there no pitfalls on the way?" I asked.

"There is one. The most dreadful of all sins: spiritual arrogance. If love opens your heart to deeper understanding and you misuse the light thus given by feeling superior and contempting others, then you commit the greatest sin against your true self."

He again increased his speed. Now it was seven miles an hour, and I could not follow him without running. I realized that he wished to be left alone. The Tibetan *nalliorpas* never make an *effort* to be "kind". They do not hesitate to be firm if they wish to bring an interview to a conclusion.

I stopped for a moment and looked behind me. When I turned again a few seconds later he was no longer in sight. This was perhaps my strangest experience during my travels in Asia.

Now he was alone again physically, but telepathically he was probably in contact with all corners of the universe. Imagine a man knowing so much, and being so immeasurably wise, and yet being unable to help his fellow creatures directly.

These men never try to influence other people's free-will. Life would have no meaning if we just became puppets, automatically following the dictates of spiritual leaders, be they ever so wise and powerful. Man has the choice between the greatest good and the most horrible evil. His fate lies in his own hands. That is the glory of man. Some day he will save himself by his own effort and become like the wise men of Tibet. They are analogous to signposts. They say so themselves.

Man creates his own limitations. He himself must destroy the things he has created. The hermits could demonstrate to children how they walk, but if they carried them in their arms, the children would never learn to walk.

The real hermits are beyond criticism. They do not care whether they are praised or blamed. The opinion of other people, which to most Tibetans is so important that their whole lives bear the stamp of the automatic thoughts and prejudices of the epoch in which they happen to live, does not seem to influence the wise men of Tibet in any way.

These spontaneously unselfish men, who do not make any virtue of their unselfishness, but who are continually and effortlessly kind and compassionate, seem to have conquered death. They are "eternal", seeing that the very notion of time only exists in so far as the individual draws a border-line between the "I" and the "non-I", and considers everything in relation to his little self.

And as they are "eternal" in the above sense, these men are not afraid of death, although their "I" does not believe in any particular personal paradise where it would be comfortably housed.

However, these men are fully conscious of being distinct and separate entities and *do not give up their Soul.* They are and remain *strong personalities* who work out of love for others.

And this is *Nirvana, real* Nirvana, about which so many false notions prevail, not only in Western countries, but also in the East, as real Nirvana is very often mistaken for so-called Nirvana which is a fabrication of the priests. False Nirvana is an abolishment and negation of life, but *real Nirvana* is its full unfoldment by the spiritualization of matter, instead of running away from it or over-emphasizing its importance.

Real Nirvana is a state in which man is everything and nothing at the same time. It is a state of being past death, past the fear of death. This replacing of the *boundless selfishness* of the "I" by a voluntarily limited selfishness is not annihilation but *a different state of consciousness.* Such an "I" puts itself *voluntarily* at the disposal of the world and works for the world, because it feels one with all the joys and sorrows of the world and not because it is promised some selfish reward, be it ever so subtle.

To understand the full significance of real Nirvana, it must be approached with the brain *and* the heart. It cannot be dissected like a dead flower, as real Nirvana is a *living reality*.

There is a reference to real Nirvana also in the New Testament. "The Kingdom of Heaven is not here or there. It is within you." Real heaven is the utter disappearance of self-centredness in the widest sense of the word.

The wise men of Tibet never call themselves Buddhists or claim that they are successors or representatives of Buddha. They could join hands with the very few real Christians who live the spirit of the Bible continually *in the little things of their daily lives*.

Buddha brought a great and radiant light. By giving people a little *"ersatz"* light, his self-styled representatives entirely defeat the purpose of the living Buddha. If all these false lights did not exist and there was utter darkness spiritually, people as individuals would step forth and seek the real light which shines forth everywhere radiantly and gratuitously, if we only open our hearts and minds to it.

There is an enormous difference between the majority of so-called Buddhists, with the idea of a so-called Nirvana dangling before their eyes and leading them away from matter, and the few wise men of Tibet who *are* in a state of real Nirvana here on earth. The latter fully realize spirit in matter. With these men, religion is a constructive and living thing, and not a means of making people weak and sheepish.

Dogmatic Buddhism is an organized distortion of the spirit of the living Buddha.

Will it be so for ever, or will *real spirituality* be realized some day in Tibet?

Asia is at the cross-roads. Mankind is at the cross-roads. A new conception of life is needed if this world is not to perish.

"There is the alternative between vertiginous summits and dreadful chasms." Such were the words used by one of the wise men of Tibet. This not only applies to the fate of individuals, but also to the destiny of Humanity.

The signs of the times herald a new age. It is close at hand. Will it be better, will it be even more dreadful than the present one? The precipice is within inches of the summit. Every one of us contributes in a certain measure to the course events will take. Let us be conscious of our responsibility.

The wise men of Tibet watch events, but as they say themselves, they are mere signposts. They do not interfere with people's free-will, for man is essentially free to choose his way to radiant light or utter darkness. That is where his glory lies.

The more we learn spiritually the greater our responsibility. There is a spark of selfless love embedded in the innermost recess of our hearts. It keeps us in harmony with our Soul, our true self. If this Soul guides us, Love without any thought of a spiritual reward is the guiding principle of our lives, and every increase in knowledge and power is automatically balanced by a corresponding increase in our sense of responsibility and Humility.

This is the supreme lesson I learned while studying the spiritual life of Tibet.

THE END

TIBETAN LAMA BAND

T. ILLION

Rätselhaftes Tibet

In Verkleidung unter Lamas,
Räubern und wahrhaft Weisen

Uranus-Verlag Max Duphorn · Hamburg 24

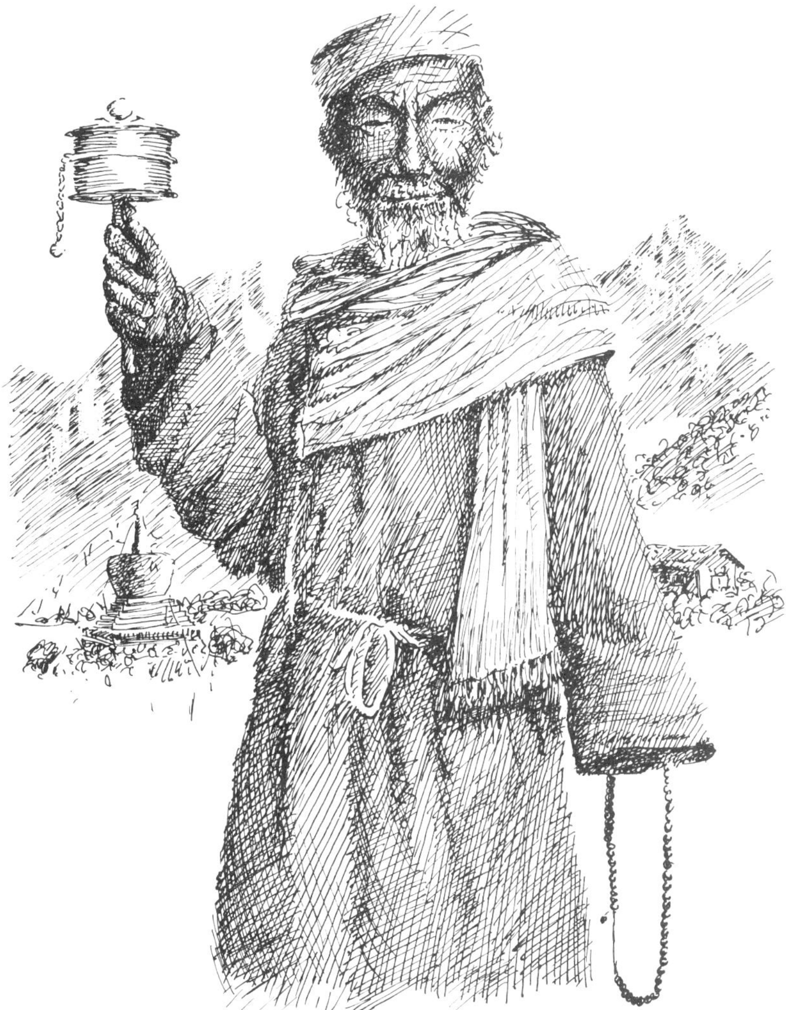

The sacred mountain Chomo Lhari in the frontier district of Bhutan
Lamas blowing sacred horns on the roof of the medical faculty lCags-po-ri

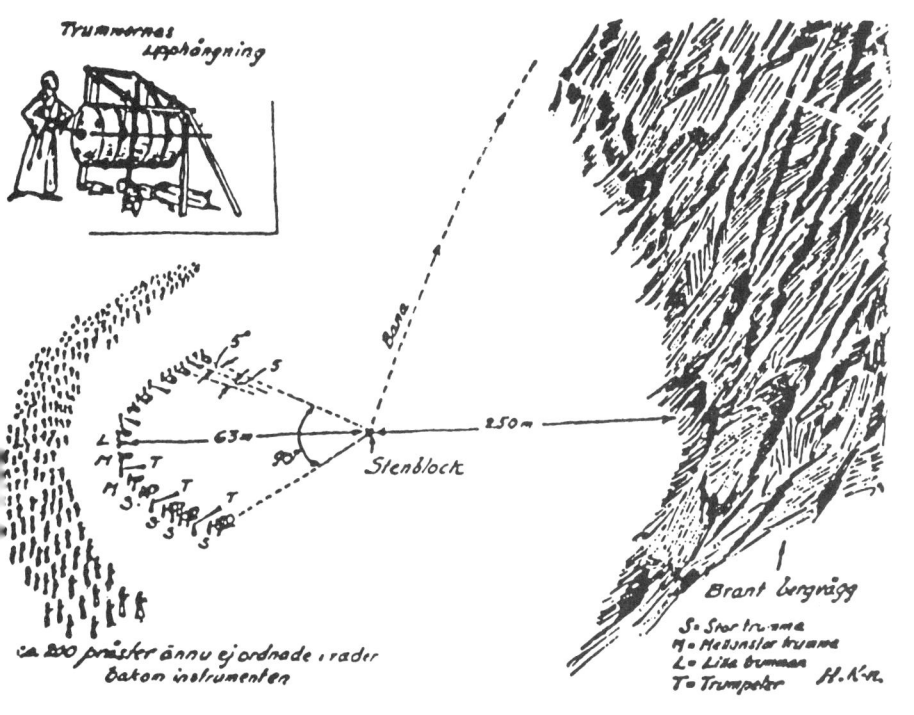

Monastery construction, Tibetan style according to Swedish Designer Henry Kjellson. The steep mountain side is on the right. In the centre is the stone block, and on the left are the priests and musicians. S=big drum, M=medium drum, T=trumpeter. Inset shows method of suspending drum, and gives an idea of its size. As shown here, Kjellson says, the 200 priests are waiting to take up their positions in straight lines of 8 or 10 behind the instruments, 'like spokes in a wheel.' Unlikely as it may seem, this operation has an intriguing precision, made slightly more so by Kjellson's meticulously detailed description.

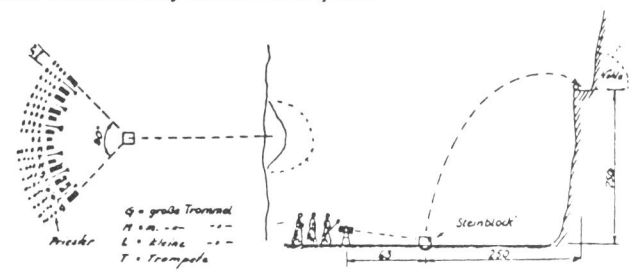

Tibetan Monks levitate stones by using an acoustic levitation technique with the aid of drums in this 1939 sketch by Swedish aircraft designer Henry Kjellson.

Modern Chinese acrobats and illusionists trace their traditions back at least to the arrival of Near Eastern conjurors during Han and Roman times. (From *Zeldzaame Reizen*... by Edward Melton, Amsterdam, 1702, reprinted in Yule's *Marco Polo*)

Potala Palace of Lhasa during the yearly festival of Losar.

Tibetan men with their horses. Amdo, Tibet, circa 1930.
Photographed by M. C. Griebenow.

The Fourteenth Dalai Lama with the teenage king of Bhutan.

LOST CITIES OF ATLANTIS, ANCIENT EUROPE & THE MEDITERRANEAN
by David Hatcher Childress
Atlantis! The legendary lost continent comes under the close scrutiny of maverick archaeologist David Hatcher Childress in this sixth book in the internationally popular *Lost Cities* series. Childress takes the reader in search of sunken cities in the Mediterranean; across the Atlas Mountains in search of Atlantean ruins; to remote islands in search of megalithic ruins; to meet living legends and secret societies. From Ireland to Turkey, Morocco to Eastern Europe, and around the remote islands of the Mediterranean and Atlantic, Childress takes the reader on an astonishing quest for mankind's past. Ancient technology, cataclysms, megalithic construction, lost civilizations and devastating wars of the past are all explored in this book. Childress challenges the skeptics and proves that great civilizations not only existed in the past, but the modern world and its problems are reflections of the ancient world of Atlantis.
524 PAGES. 6x9 PAPERBACK. ILLUSTRATED. BIBLIOGRAPHY & INDEX. $16.95. CODE: MED

LOST CITIES OF ANCIENT LEMURIA & THE PACIFIC
by David Hatcher Childress
Was there once a continent in the Pacific? Called Lemuria or Pacifica by geologists, Mu or Pan by the mystics, there is now ample mythological, geological and archaeological evidence to "prove" that an advanced and ancient civilization once lived in the central Pacific. Maverick archaeologist and explorer David Hatcher Childress combs the Indian Ocean, Australia and the Pacific in search of the surprising truth about mankind's past. Contains photos of the underwater city on Pohnpei; explanations on how the statues were levitated around Easter Island in a clockwise vortex movement; tales of disappearing islands; Egyptians in Australia; and more.
379 PAGES. 6x9 PAPERBACK. ILLUSTRATED. FOOTNOTES & BIBLIOGRAPHY. $14.95. CODE: LEM

LOST CITIES & ANCIENT MYSTERIES OF SOUTH AMERICA
by David Hatcher Childress
Rogue adventurer and maverick archaeologist David Hatcher Childress takes the reader on unforgettable journeys deep into deadly jungles, high up on windswept mountains and across scorching deserts in search of lost civilizations and ancient mysteries. Travel with David and explore stone cities high in mountain forests and hear fantastic tales of Inca treasure, living dinosaurs, and a mysterious tunnel system. Whether he is hopping freight trains, searching for secret cities, or just dealing with the daily problems of food, money, and romance, the author keeps the reader spellbound. Includes both early and current maps, photos, and illustrations, and plenty of advice for the explorer planning his or her own journey of discovery.
381 PAGES. 6x9 PAPERBACK. ILLUSTRATED. FOOTNOTES. BIBLIOGRAPHY. INDEX. $16.95. CODE: SAM

LOST CITIES & ANCIENT MYSTERIES OF AFRICA & ARABIA
by David Hatcher Childress
Across ancient deserts, dusty plains and steaming jungles, maverick archaeologist David Childress continues his world-wide quest for lost cities and ancient mysteries. Join him as he discovers forbidden cities in the Empty Quarter of Arabia; "Atlantean" ruins in Egypt and the Kalahari desert; a mysterious, ancient empire in the Sahara; and more. This is the tale of an extraordinary life on the road: across war-torn countries, Childress searches for King Solomon's Mines, living dinosaurs, the Ark of the Covenant and the solutions to some of the fantastic mysteries of the past.
423 PAGES. 6x9 PAPERBACK. ILLUSTRATED. FOOTNOTES & BIBLIOGRAPHY. $14.95. CODE: AFA

LOST CITIES OF NORTH & CENTRAL AMERICA
by David Hatcher Childress
Down the back roads from coast to coast, maverick archaeologist and adventurer David Hatcher Childress goes deep into unknown America. With this incredible book, you will search for lost Mayan cities and books of gold, discover an ancient canal system in Arizona, climb gigantic pyramids in the Midwest, explore megalithic monuments in New England, and join the astonishing quest for lost cities throughout North America. From the war-torn jungles of Guatemala, Nicaragua and Honduras to the deserts, mountains and fields of Mexico, Canada, and the U.S.A., Childress takes the reader in search of sunken ruins, Viking forts, strange tunnel systems, living dinosaurs, early Chinese explorers, and fantastic lost treasure. Packed with both early and current maps, photos and illustrations.
590 PAGES. 6x9 PAPERBACK. ILLUSTRATED. FOOTNOTES. BIBLIOGRAPHY. INDEX. $16.95. CODE: NCA

LOST CITIES OF CHINA, CENTRAL INDIA & ASIA
by David Hatcher Childress
Like a real life "Indiana Jones," maverick archaeologist David Childress takes the reader on an incredible adventure across some of the world's oldest and most remote countries in search of lost cities and ancient mysteries. Discover ancient cities in the Gobi Desert; hear fantastic tales of lost continents, vanished civilizations and secret societies bent on ruling the world; visit forgotten monasteries in forbidding snow-capped mountains with strange tunnels to mysterious subterranean cities! A unique combination of far-out exploration and practical travel advice, it will astound and delight the experienced traveler or the armchair voyager.
429 PAGES. 6x9 PAPERBACK. ILLUSTRATED. FOOTNOTES & BIBLIOGRAPHY. $14.95. CODE: CHI

TECHNOLOGY OF THE GODS
The Incredible Sciences of the Ancients
by David Hatcher Childress

Popular *Lost Cities* author David Hatcher Childress takes us into the amazing world of ancient technology, from computers in antiquity to the "flying machines of the gods." Childress looks at the technology that was allegedly used in Atlantis and the theory that the Great Pyramid of Egypt was originally a gigantic power station. He examines tales of ancient flight and the technology that it involved; how the ancients used electricity; megalithic building techniques; the use of crystal lenses and the fire from the gods; evidence of various high tech weapons in the past, including atomic weapons; ancient metallurgy and heavy machinery; the role of modern inventors such as Nikola Tesla in bringing ancient technology back into modern use; impossible artifacts; and more.
356 PAGES. 6x9 PAPERBACK. ILLUSTRATED. BIBLIOGRAPHY. $16.95. CODE: TGOD

VIMANA AIRCRAFT OF ANCIENT INDIA & ATLANTIS
by David Hatcher Childress, introduction by Ivan T. Sanderson

Did the ancients have the technology of flight? In this incredible volume on ancient India, authentic Indian texts such as the *Ramayana* and the *Mahabharata* are used to prove that ancient aircraft were in use more than four thousand years ago. Included in this book is the entire Fourth Century BC manuscript *Vimaanika Shastra* by the ancient author Maharishi Bharadwaaja, translated into English by the Mysore Sanskrit professor G.R. Josyer. Also included are chapters on Atlantean technology, the incredible Rama Empire of India and the devastating wars that destroyed it. Also an entire chapter on mercury vortex propulsion and mercury gyros, the power source described in the ancient Indian texts. Not to be missed by those interested in ancient civilizations or the UFO enigma.
334 PAGES. 6x9 PAPERBACK. ILLUSTRATED. $15.95. CODE: VAA

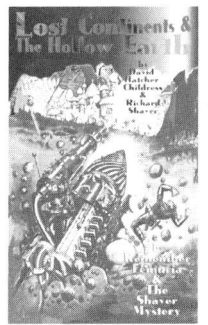

LOST CONTINENTS & THE HOLLOW EARTH
I Remember Lemuria and the Shaver Mystery
by David Hatcher Childress & Richard Shaver

Lost Continents & the Hollow Earth is Childress' thorough examination of the early hollow earth stories of Richard Shaver and the fascination that fringe fantasy subjects such as lost continents and the hollow earth have had for the American public. Shaver's rare 1948 book *I Remember Lemuria* is reprinted in its entirety, and the book is packed with illustrations from Ray Palmer's *Amazing Stories* magazine of the 1940s. Palmer and Shaver told of tunnels running through the earth—tunnels inhabited by the Deros and Teros, humanoids from an ancient spacefaring race that had inhabited the earth, eventually going underground, hundreds of thousands of years ago. Childress discusses the famous hollow earth books and delves deep into whatever reality may be behind the stories of tunnels in the earth. Operation High Jump to Antarctica in 1947 and Admiral Byrd's bizarre statements, tunnel systems in South America and Tibet, the underground world of Agartha, the belief of UFOs coming from the South Pole, more.
344 PAGES. 6x9 PAPERBACK. ILLUSTRATED. $16.95. CODE: LCHE

A HITCHHIKER'S GUIDE TO ARMAGEDDON
by David Hatcher Childress
With wit and humor, popular Lost Cities author David Hatcher Childress takes us around the world and back in his trippy finalé to the Lost Cities series. He's off on an adventure in search of the apocalypse and end times. Childress hits the road from the fortress of Megiddo, the legendary citadel in northern Israel where Armageddon is prophesied to start. Hitchhiking around the world, Childress takes us from one adventure to another, to ancient cities in the deserts and the legends of worlds before our own. Childress muses on the rise and fall of civilizations, and the forces that have shaped mankind over the millennia, including wars, invasions and cataclysms. He discusses the ancient Armageddons of the past, and chronicles recent Middle East developments and their ominous undertones. In the meantime, he becomes a cargo cult god on a remote island off New Guinea, gets dragged into the Kennedy Assassination by one of the "conspirators," investigates a strange power operating out of the Altai Mountains of Mongolia, and discovers how the Knights Templar and their off-shoots have driven the world toward an epic battle centered around Jerusalem and the Middle East.
320 pages. 6x9 Paperback. Illustrated. Bibliography. Index. $16.95. code: HGA

IN QUEST OF LOST WORLDS
by Count Byron Khun de Prorok
Finally, a reprint of Count Byron de Prorok's classic archeology/adventure book first published in 1936 by E.P. Dutton & Co. in New York. In this exciting and well illustrated book, de Prorok takes us into the deep Sahara of forbidden Algeria, to unknown Ethiopia, and to the many prehistoric ruins of the Yucatan. Includes: Tin Hinan, Legendary Queen of the Tuaregs; The mysterious A'Haggar Range of southern Algeria; Jupiter, Ammon and Tripolitania; The "Talking Dune"; The Land of the Garamantes; Mexico and the Poison Trail; Seeking Atlantis—Chichen Itza; Shadowed by the "Little People"—the Lacandon Pygmie Maya; Ancient Pyramids of the Usamasinta and Piedras Negras in Guatemala; In Search of King Solomon's Mines & the Land of Ophir; Ancient Emerald Mines of Ethiopia. Also included in this book are 24 pages of special illustrations of the famous—and strange—wall paintings of the Ahaggar from the rare book *The Search for the Tassili Frescoes* by Henri Lhote (1959). A visual treat of a remote area of the world that is even today forbidden to outsiders!
324 pages. 6x9 Paperback. Illustrated. $16.95. code: IQLW

THE LAND OF OSIRIS
An Introduction to Khemitology
by Stephen S. Mehler
Was there an advanced prehistoric civilization in ancient Egypt? Were they the people who built the great pyramids and carved the Great Sphinx? Did the pyramids serve as energy devices and not as tombs for kings? Mehler has uncovered an indigenous oral tradition that still exists in Egypt, and has been fortunate to have studied with a living master of this tradition, Abd'El Hakim Awyan. Mehler has also been given permission to present these teachings to the Western world, teachings that unfold a whole new understanding of ancient Egypt and have only been presented heretofore in fragments by other researchers. Chapters include: Egyptology and Its Paradigms; Khemitology—New Paradigms; Asgat Nefer—The Harmony of Water; Khemit and the Myth of Atlantis; The Extraterrestrial Question; more.
272 pages. 6x9 Paperback. Illustrated. Color Section. Bibliography. $18.95. code: LOOS

THE MYSTERY OF EASTER ISLAND
by Katherine Routledge
The reprint of Katherine Routledge's classic archaeology book which was first published in London in 1919. The book details her journey by yacht from England to South America, around Patagonia to Chile and on to Easter Island. Routledge explored the amazing island and produced one of the first-ever accounts of the life, history and legends of this strange and remote place. Routledge discusses the statues, pyramid-platforms, Rongo Rongo script, the Bird Cult, the war between the Short Ears and the Long Ears, the secret caves, ancient roads on the island, and more. This rare book serves as a sourcebook on the early discoveries and theories on Easter Island.

432 PAGES. 6X9 PAPERBACK. ILLUSTRATED. $16.95. CODE: MEI

IN SECRET TIBET
by Theodore Illion
Reprint of a rare 30s adventure travel book. Illion was a German wayfarer who not only spoke fluent Tibetan, but travelled in disguise as a native through forbidden Tibet when it was off-limits to all outsiders. His incredible adventures make this one of the most exciting travel books ever published. Includes illustrations of Tibetan monks levitating stones by acoustics.

210 PAGES. 5X9 PAPERBACK. ILLUSTRATED. $15.95. CODE: IST

DARKNESS OVER TIBET
by Theodore Illion
In this second reprint of Illion's rare books, the German traveller continues his journey through Tibet and is given directions to a strange underground city. As the original publisher's remarks said, "this is a rare account of an underground city in Tibet by the only Westerner ever to enter it and escape alive!"

210 PAGES. 5X9 PAPERBACK. ILLUSTRATED. $15.95. CODE: DOT

MYSTERY CITIES OF THE MAYA
Exploration and Adventure in Belize
by Thomas Gann
First published in 1925, *Mystery Cities of the Maya* is a classic in Central American archaeology-adventure. Gann was close friends with Mike Mitchell-Hedges, the British adventurer who discovered the famous crystal skull with his adopted daughter Sammy and Lady Richmond Brown, their benefactress. Gann battles pirates along Belize's coast and goes upriver with Mitchell-Hedges to the site of Lubaantun where they excavate a strange lost city where the crystal skull was discovered. Lubaantun is a unique city in the Mayan world as it is built out of precisely carved blocks of stone without the usual plaster-cement facing. Lubaantun contained several large pyramids partially destroyed by earthquakes and a large amount of artifacts. Gann shared Mitchell-Hedges belief in Atlantis and lost civilizations (pre-Mayan) in Central America and the Caribbean. Lots of good photos, maps and diagrams.

252 PAGES. 6X9 PAPERBACK. ILLUSTRATED. $16.95. CODE: MCOM

IN SECRET MONGOLIA
by Henning Haslund
First published by Kegan Paul of London in 1934, Haslund takes us into the barely known world of Mongolia of 1921, a land of god-kings, bandits, vast mountain wilderness and a Russian army running amok. Starting in Peking, Haslund journeys to Mongolia as part of the Krebs Expedition—a mission to establish a Danish butter farm in a remote corner of northern Mongolia. Along the way, he smuggles guns and nitroglycerin, is thrown into a prison by the new Communist regime, battles the Robber Princess and more. With Haslund we meet the "Mad Baron" Ungern-Sternberg and his renegade Russian army, the many characters of Urga's fledgling foreign community, and the last god-king of Mongolia, Seng Chen Gegen, the fifth reincarnation of the Tiger god and the "ruler of all Torguts." Aside from the esoteric and mystical material, there is plenty of just plain adventure: Haslund encounters a Mongolian werewolf; is ambushed along the trail; escapes from prison and fights terrifying blizzards; more.

374 PAGES. 6x9 PAPERBACK. ILLUSTRATED. BIBLIOGRAPHY & INDEX. $16.95. CODE: **ISM**

MEN & GODS IN MONGOLIA
by Henning Haslund
First published in 1935 by Kegan Paul of London, Haslund takes us to the lost city of Karakota in the Gobi desert. We meet the Bodgo Gegen, a god-king in Mongolia similar to the Dalai Lama of Tibet. We meet Dambin Jansang, the dreaded warlord of the "Black Gobi." There is even material in this incredible book on the Hi-mori, an "airhorse" that flies through the sky (similar to a Vimana) and carries with it the sacred stone of Chintamani. Aside from the esoteric and mystical material, there is plenty of just plain adventure: Haslund and companions journey across the Gobi desert by camel caravan; are kidnapped and held for ransom; witness initiation into Shamanic societies; meet reincarnated warlords; and experience the violent birth of "modern" Mongolia.

358 PAGES. 6x9 PAPERBACK. ILLUSTRATED. BIBLIOGRAPHY & INDEX. $16.95. CODE: **MGM**

MYSTERIES OF ANCIENT SOUTH AMERICA
Atlantis Reprint Series
by Harold T. Wilkins
The reprint of Wilkins' classic book on the megaliths and mysteries of South America. This book predates Wilkin's book *Secret Cities of Old South America* published in 1952. *Mysteries of Ancient South America* was first published in 1947 and is considered a classic book of its kind. With diagrams, photos and maps, Wilkins digs into old manuscripts and books to bring us some truly amazing stories of South America: a bizarre subterranean tunnel system; lost cities in the remote border jungles of Brazil; legends of Atlantis in South America; cataclysmic changes that shaped South America; and other strange stories from one of the world's great researchers. Chapters include: Our Earth's Greatest Disaster, Dead Cities of Ancient Brazil, The Jungle Light that Shines by Itself, The Missionary Men in Black: Forerunners of the Great Catastrophe, The Sign of the Sun: The World's Oldest Alphabet, Sign-Posts to the Shadow of Atlantis, The Atlanean "Subterraneans" of the Incas, Tiahuanacu and the Giants, more.

236 PAGES. 6x9 PAPERBACK. ILLUSTRATED. INDEX. $14.95. CODE: **MASA**

SECRET CITIES OF OLD SOUTH AMERICA
by Harold T. Wilkins
The reprint of Wilkins' classic book, first published in 1952, claiming that South America was Atlantis. Chapters include Mysteries of a Lost World; Atlantis Unveiled; Red Riddles on the Rocks; South America's Amazons Existed!; The Mystery of El Dorado and Gran Payatiti—the Final Refuge of the Incas; Monstrous Beasts of the Unexplored Swamps & Wilds; Weird Denizens of Antediluvian Forests; New Light on Atlantis from the World's Oldest Book; The Mystery of Old Man Noah and the Arks; and more.
438 PAGES. 6X9 PAPERBACK. ILLUSTRATED. BIBLIOGRAPHY & INDEX. $16.95. CODE: SCOS

THE SHADOW OF ATLANTIS
The Echoes of Atlantean Civilization Tracked through Space & Time
by Colonel Alexander Braghine
First published in 1940, *The Shadow of Atlantis* is one of the great classics of Atlantis research. The book amasses a great deal of archaeological, anthropological, historical and scientific evidence in support of a lost continent in the Atlantic Ocean. Braghine covers such diverse topics as Egyptians in Central America, the myth of Quetzalcoatl, the Basque language and its connection with Atlantis, the connections with the ancient pyramids of Mexico, Egypt and Atlantis, the sudden demise of mammoths, legends of giants and much more. Braghine was a linguist and spends part of the book tracing ancient languages to Atlantis and studying little-known inscriptions in Brazil, deluge myths and the connections between ancient languages. Braghine takes us on a fascinating journey through space and time in search of the lost continent.
288 PAGES. 6X9 PAPERBACK. ILLUSTRATED. $16.95. CODE: SOA

ATLANTIS: MOTHER OF EMPIRES
Atlantis Reprint Series
by Robert Stacy-Judd
Robert Stacy-Judd's classic 1939 book on Atlantis is back in print in this large-format paperback edition. Stacy-Judd was a California architect and an expert on the Mayas and their relationship to Atlantis. He was an excellent artist and his work is lavishly illustrated. The eighteen comprehensive chapters in the book are: The Mayas and the Lost Atlantis; Conjectures and Opinions; The Atlantean Theory; Cro-Magnon Man; East is West; And West is East; The Mormons and the Mayas; Astrology in Two Hemispheres; The Language of Architecture; The American Indian; Pre-Panamanians and Pre-Incas; Columns and City Planning; Comparisons and Mayan Art; The Iberian Link; The Maya Tongue; Quetzalcoatl; Summing Up the Evidence; The Mayas in Yucatan.
340 PAGES. 8X11 PAPERBACK. ILLUSTRATED. INDEX. $19.95. CODE: AMOE

ATLANTIS IN SPAIN
A Study of the Ancient Sun Kingdoms of Spain
by E.M. Whishaw
First published by Rider & Co. of London in 1928, this classic book is a study of the megaliths of Spain, ancient writing, cyclopean walls, sun worshipping empires, hydraulic engineering, and sunken cities. An extremely rare book, it was out of print for 60 years. Learn about the Biblical Tartessus; an Atlantean city at Niebla; the Temple of Hercules and the Sun Temple of Seville; Libyans and the Copper Age; more. Profusely illustrated with photos, maps and drawings.
284 PAGES. 6X9 PAPERBACK. ILLUSTRATED. $15.95. CODE: AIS

THE HISTORY OF ATLANTIS
by Lewis Spence
Lewis Spence's classic book on Atlantis is now back in print! Spence was a Scottish historian (1874-1955) who is best known for his volumes on world mythology and his five Atlantis books. *The History of Atlantis* (1926) is considered his finest. Spence does his scholarly best in chapters on the Sources of Atlantean History, the Geography of Atlantis, the Races of Atlantis, the Kings of Atlantis, the Religion of Atlantis, the Colonies of Atlantis, more. Sixteen chapters in all.
240 PAGES. 6X9 PAPERBACK. ILLUSTRATED WITH MAPS, PHOTOS & DIAGRAMS. $16.95. CODE: HOA

PIRATES & THE LOST TEMPLAR FLEET
The Secret Naval War Between the Templars & the Vatican
by David Hatcher Childress
The lost Templar fleet was originally based at La Rochelle in southern France, but fled to the deep fiords of Scotland upon the dissolution of the Order by King Phillip. This banned fleet of ships was later commanded by the St. Clair family of Rosslyn Chapel (birthplace of Free Masonry). St. Clair and his Templars made a voyage to Canada in the year 1398 AD, nearly 100 years before Columbus! Chapters include: 10,000 Years of Seafaring; The Knights Templar & the Crusades; The Templars and the Assassins; The Lost Templar Fleet and the Jolly Roger; Maps of the Ancient Sea Kings; Pirates, Templars and the New World; Christopher Columbus—Secret Templar Pirate?; Later Day Pirates and the War with the Vatican; Pirate Utopias and the New Jerusalem; more.
320 PAGES. 6X9 PAPERBACK. ILLUSTRATED. BIBLIOGRAPHY. $16.95. CODE: PLTF

RIDDLE OF THE PACIFIC
by John Macmillan Brown
Oxford scholar Brown's classic work on lost civilizations of the Pacific is now back in print! John Macmillan Brown was an historian and New Zealand's premier scientist when he wrote about the origins of the Maoris. After many years of travel thoughout the Pacific studying the people and customs of the south seas islands, he wrote *Riddle of the Pacific* in 1924. The book is packed with rare turn-of-the-century illustrations. Don't miss Brown's classic study of Easter Island, ancient scripts, megalithic roads and cities, more. Brown was an early believer in a lost continent in the Pacific.
460 PAGES. 6x9 PAPERBACK. ILLUSTRATED. $16.95.
CODE: SOA

MAPS OF THE ANCIENT SEA KINGS
Evidence of Advanced Civilization in the Ice Age
by Charles H. Hapgood
Charles Hapgood's classic 1966 book on ancient maps produces concrete evidence of an advanced world-wide civilization existing many thousands of years before ancient Egypt. He has found the evidence in the Piri Reis Map that shows Antarctica, the Hadji Ahmed map, the Oronteus Finaeus and other amazing maps. Hapgood concluded that these maps were made from more ancient maps from the various ancient archives around the world, now lost. Not only were these unknown people more advanced in mapmaking than any people prior to the 18th century, it appears they mapped all the continents. The Americas were mapped thousands of years before Columbus. Antarctica was mapped when its coasts were free of ice.
316 PAGES. 7x10 PAPERBACK. ILLUSTRATED. BIBLIOGRAPHY & INDEX. $19.95. CODE: MASK

PATH OF THE POLE
by Charles Hapgood
Hapgood researched Antarctica, ancient maps and the geological record to conclude that the Earth's crust has slipped in the inner core many times in the past, changing the position of the pole. *Path of the Pole* discusses the various "pole shifts" in Earth's past, giving evidence for each one, and moves on to possible future pole shifts. Packed with illustrations, this is the sourcebook for many other books on cataclysms and pole shifts.
356 PAGES. 6x9 PAPERBACK. ILLUSTRATED. $16.95. CODE: POP

THE ORION PROPHECY
Egyptian & Mayan Prophecies on the Cataclysm of 2012
by Patrick Geryl and Gino Ratinckx
In the year 2012 the Earth awaits a super catastrophe: its magnetic field will reverse in one go. Phenomenal earthquakes and tidal waves will completely destroy our civilization. Europe and North America will shift thousands of kilometers northwards into polar climes. These dire predictions stem from the Mayans and Egyptians—descendants of the legendary Atlantis. The Atlanteans had highly evolved astronomical knowledge and were able to exactly predict the previous world-wide flood in 9792 BC. They built tens of thousands of boats and escaped to South America and Egypt. In the year 2012 Venus, Orion and several others stars will take the same 'code-positions' as in 9792 BC! For thousands of years historical sources have told of a forgotten time capsule of ancient wisdom located in a labyrinth of secret chambers filled with artifacts and documents from the previous flood.
324 PAGES. 6x9 PAPERBACK. ILLUSTRATED. $16.95. CODE: ORP

ORDERING INSTRUCTIONS

✓ Remit by USD$ Check, Money Order or Credit Card
✓ Visa, Master Card, Discover & AmEx Accepted
✓ Prices May Change Without Notice
✓ 10% Discount for 3 or more Items

SHIPPING CHARGES

United States

✓ Postal Book Rate { $3.00 First Item / 50¢ Each Additional Item
✓ Priority Mail { $4.50 First Item / $2.00 Each Additional Item
✓ UPS { $5.00 First Item / $1.50 Each Additional Item
NOTE: UPS Delivery Available to Mainland USA Only

Canada

✓ Postal Book Rate { $6.00 First Item / $2.00 Each Additional Item
✓ Postal Air Mail { $8.00 First Item / $2.50 Each Additional Item
✓ Personal Checks or Bank Drafts MUST BE USD$ and Drawn on a US Bank
✓ Canadian Postal Money Orders OK
✓ Payment MUST BE USD$

All Other Countries

✓ Surface Delivery { $10.00 First Item / $4.00 Each Additional Item
✓ Postal Air Mail { $14.00 First Item / $5.00 Each Additional Item
✓ Payment MUST BE USD$
✓ Checks and Money Orders MUST BE USD$ and Drawn on a US Bank or branch.
✓ Add $5.00 for Air Mail Subscription to Future *Adventures Unlimited* Catalogs

SPECIAL NOTES

✓ RETAILERS: Standard Discounts Available
✓ BACKORDERS: We Backorder all Out-of-Stock Items Unless Otherwise Requested
✓ PRO FORMA INVOICES: Available on Request

One Adventure Place
P.O. Box 74
Kempton, Illinois 60946
United States of America
Tel.: 815-253-6390 • Fax: 815-253-6300
Email: auphq@frontiernet.net
http://www.adventuresunlimitedpress.com
or www.adventuresunlimited.nl

Please check: ✓

☐ This is my first order   ☐ I have ordered before

Name
Address
City
State/Province _____ Postal Code _____
Country
Phone day _____ Evening _____
Fax

Item Code	Item Description	Qty	Total

Please check: ✓

Subtotal ▶
Less Discount-10% for 3 or more items ▶

☐ Postal-Surface   Balance ▶
☐ Postal-Air Mail Illinois Residents 6.25% Sales Tax ▶
   (Priority in USA)   Previous Credit ▶
☐ UPS   Shipping ▶
   (Mainland USA only) Total (check/MO in USD$ only) ▶

☐ Visa/MasterCard/Discover/Amex

Card Number
Expiration Date

10% Discount When You Order 3 or More Items!